COMMON CORE STANDARDS

STANDARDS

for | High School Mathematics

A QUICK-START GUIDE

Edited by John Kendall

COMMON CORE
STANDARDS

for | High School Mathematics

Amitra Schwols

Kathleen Dempsey

Alexandria, Virginia USA

Mid-continent Research for Education and Learning
Denver, Colorado USA

1703 N. Beauregard St. • Alexandria, VA 22311-1714 USA
Phone: 800-933-2723 or 703-578-9600 • Fax: 703-575-5400
Website: www.ascd.org • E-mail: member@ascd.org
Author guidelines: www.ascd.org/write

MCREL

Mid-continent Research for Education and Learning
4601 DTC Boulevard, Suite 500
Denver, CO 80237 USA
Phone: 303-337-0990 • Fax: 303-337-3005
Website: www.mcrel.org • E-mail: info@mcrel.org

PAPERBACK ISBN: 978-1-4166-1462-3   ASCD product #113011   n11/12

Also available as an e-book (see Books in Print for the ISBNs).

Quantity discounts: 10–49 copies, 10%; 50+ copies, 15%; for 1,000 or more copies,
call 800-933-2723, ext. 5634, or 703-575-5634. For desk copies: www.ascd.org/deskcopy.

Library of Congress Cataloging-in-Publication Data
Schwols, Amitra.
  Common core standards for high school mathematics : a quick-start guide / Amitra Schwols
and Kathleen Dempsey.
     pages cm
  Includes bibliographical references.
  ISBN 978-1-4166-1462-3 (pbk. : alk. paper)
  1. Mathematics–Study and teaching (Secondary)–Standards. I. Dempsey, Kathleen, 1952- II. Title.
  QA11.2.S39 2012
  510.71′273—dc23
                             2012033784

22 21 20 19 18 17 16 15 14 13 12   1 2 3 4 5 6 7 8 9 10 11 12

COMMON CORE STANDARDS

for | High School Mathematics

Acknowledgments

We would like to acknowledge Kirsten Miller and John Kendall for their crucial role in making our thoughts much more readable; Greg Gallagher and the North Dakota Curriculum Initiative committee, who provided us with valuable insights into the challenges facing teachers as they begin to work with the Common Core standards; Ceri Dean for her step-by-step guide to lesson planning; Amber Evenson and Ann Zingraff-Newton for their collaboration and content expertise in developing the lessons; our McREL colleagues, who provided an analytical ear as we discussed the work; and our families, for supporting us as we worked on this project.

Introduction

In July 2009, nearly all state school superintendents and the nation's governors joined in an effort to identify a common set of standards in mathematics and English language arts (ELA), with the goal of providing a clear, shared set of expectations that would prepare students for success in both college and career. The Common Core State Standards Initiative (CCSSI) brought together researchers, academics, teachers, and others who routed multiple drafts of the standards to representatives including curriculum directors, content specialists, and technical advisors from all participating state departments of education. By spring 2010, drafts were submitted for comment to the national subject-area organizations and posted for public comment. In June 2010, the final versions were posted to a dedicated website: www.corestandards.org. (A minor update of the standards was posted in October 2010.)

At press time, 45 states, as well as Washington, D.C., and two territories, have adopted the Common Core State Standards (CCSS) for mathematics. (Minnesota has adopted the ELA standards but not the mathematics standards. Texas, Alaska, Virginia, and Nebraska have indicated that they do not plan to adopt either set, although both Virginia and Nebraska have aligned the Common Core standards with their existing standards.)

Adoption of the standards is, of course, voluntary for states and does not include a commitment to any other programs or policies. However, states that have adopted these standards will be eligible to join one of two federally funded assessment consortia that are currently tasked with developing assessments for the Common Core—the Smarter Balanced Assessment Consortium (SBAC) or the Partnership for Assessment of Readiness for College and Careers (PARCC). Sharing assessments across states promises financial relief from notoriously expensive state assessments. In addition, federal programs such as Race to the Top have required that applicants demonstrate that they have joined with other states in adopting a common set of standards and an assessment program. Although states may form new consortia, many either have opted to join or are considering joining SBAC or PARCC.

Sharing a set of standards across states offers other advantages. For example, teachers' well-designed lesson plans targeting Common Core standards will be immediately useful to a large number of colleagues. The shared language of standards should also provide teachers with more opportunities to participate in very specific discussions about content, a process that has been hampered somewhat by the variety of ways states have described virtually the same content.

For a lengthier discussion of the Common Core standards, including their link to previous standards-based education efforts and the benefits and challenges the Common Core presents, see *Understanding Common Core State Standards* (Kendall, 2011), the first booklet in this series. We also encourage readers to explore numerous resources available at corestandards.org, especially the standards document itself (CCSSI, 2010c), the document's Appendix A (CCSSI, 2010d), and the guidelines for adapting standards instruction for English language learners (CCSSI, 2010a) and students with disabilities (CCSSI, 2010b).

About This Guide

This guide is part of a series intended to further the discussion and understanding of Common Core standards on a subject-specific and grade-level basis and to provide immediate guidance to teachers who must either adapt existing lessons and activities to incorporate the Common Core or develop new lessons to teach concepts not addressed in their previous state standards.

After an overview of the general structure of the Common Core standards for high school mathematics, we consider each conceptual category in turn to examine how the standards it contains build upon and extend the skills students have acquired in earlier grades. We also explore the links between conceptual categories and domains, and we make connections between mathematical content standards and mathematical practice standards. Next, we focus on practical lesson planning with the Common Core, looking at a process for creating standards-based lessons that make the best use of the effective instructional strategies explored in *Classroom Instruction That Works,* 2nd edition (Dean, Hubbell, Pitler, & Stone, 2012). The guide concludes with an illustration of this process's outcome: three sample lessons that address Common Core standards identified as representing notable changes to high school mathematics teachers' current practice.

CHAPTER 1

About the Common Core Mathematics Standards for High School

The Common Core mathematics standards are organized into two sets: the Standards for Mathematical Content, designed to cross traditional course boundaries and cover all the conceptual mathematical understanding necessary for students to develop from kindergarten through 12th grade, and the Standards for Mathematical Practice, which highlight the kinds of procedural expertise that is essential for students to develop and use throughout this same grade span.

When first looking at the entire set of high school mathematics standards, teachers may notice several things:

- There are a lot of them (about twice the number of middle school mathematics standards).
- They are sometimes quite long, up to a paragraph in length.
- Some of the standards detail skills and concepts (e.g., reasoning, advanced statistics) that are not typically explicit in other standards documents.
- They are arranged by conceptual areas, rather than by course.

Taken together, these characteristic may seem a bit overwhelming, making it a challenge to figure out how to begin using the Common Core standards for mathematics at the high school level. In this chapter, we walk you through the standards' structure, provide an overview of how they fit together, and offer some guidance on what to focus on as you begin your implementation efforts.

The Standards for Mathematical Content

At the high school level, the Standards for Mathematical Content are organized into six "conceptual categories," specifically Number and Quantity, Algebra, Functions, Modeling, Geometry, and Statistics and Probability. Content within each of the conceptual categories is organized hierarchically as follows:

• *Domain:* Expressed in a few words, a domain articulates the big ideas within each conceptual category. For example, within the conceptual category Geometry are domains such as Congruence and Circles.

• *Cluster:* A cluster captures several ideas that, taken with all the other clusters within a domain, summarize the important aspects of that domain. For example, there are two clusters in the Circles domain. The first (Cluster A) is "Understand and apply theorems about circles," and the second (Cluster B) is "Find arc lengths and areas of sectors of circles." Content addressed in different domains and clusters may be closely related, reflecting the standards writers' emphasis on the interconnections throughout mathematics.

• *Standard:* A standard is a specific description of what students should understand and be able to do. For example, the first of four standards in the "Understand and apply theorems about circles" cluster states, "Prove that all circles are similar." A standard may be one sentence or several sentences long, and it sometimes includes lettered components. Typically, there are several standards beneath every cluster heading, although the standards themselves are numbered sequentially within the domain. The first standard in the Circles domain's Cluster B, for example, is Standard 5 within the Circles domain overall.

The conceptual category Modeling is an exception to this structure in that it is not further organized into domains, clusters, and standards. We will look more closely at that conceptual category as we delve into the implications of the structure of the Common Core.

In this guide, we will be referencing the content standards using a slightly abbreviated version of the CCSSI's official identification system, which provides a unique identifier for each standard in the Common Core and can be very useful for school staffs when developing crosswalks, planning lessons, and sharing lesson plans. Under this system, all mathematics content standards begin with the formal prefix "CCSS.Math.Content"; we have dropped this prefix in our references throughout this guide, including the sample lessons. The identification code for the high school mathematics content standards next identifies the standard as a high school standard ("HS") and then indicates the conceptual category, the domain, the cluster, and the standard number. For example, "HSA-REI.A.1" is shorthand for high school Algebra (the conceptual category), Reasoning with Equations and Inequalities (the domain name), Cluster A (the first of the domain's four clusters, identified A–D), Standard 1. "HSA-REI.A" is a shorthand way of referring to all standards in Cluster A of the Reasoning with Equations and Inequalities domain. When referencing the mathematics content standards for the lower grades, after the "CCSS.Math.Content" prefix (which, as noted above, is omitted in this guide), the specific grade level determines the first part of the code. For example, "8.G.B.6" is shorthand for Grade 8, Geometry (the domain name), Cluster B (of the domain's three clusters, identified A–C), Standard 6.

Taken as a whole, the Common Core's mathematical content standards identify what students should know and be able to do in order to be college and career ready. Note, though, that the standards document also includes some standards that may not be required of all students and are not intended for high-stakes assessment. These standards, marked with a (+), identify mathematics that students should learn in order to take advanced courses in calculus, statistics, or discrete mathematics.

The Standards for Mathematical Practice

Emphasis on students' conceptual understanding of mathematics is an aspect of the Common Core standards that sets them apart from many state standards. The eight Standards for Mathematical Practice, listed in Figure 1.1, play an important role in ensuring that students are engaged in the actual use of mathematics, not just in the acquisition of knowledge about the discipline. Indeed, the table of contents in the standards document gives equal weight to the Standards for Mathematical Practice and the Standards for Mathematical Content. This dual focus, echoed throughout the document's introductory material, has been undertaken to ensure that the standards "describe varieties of expertise that mathematics educators at all levels should seek to develop in their students" (CCSSI, 2010c, p. 6).

Figure 1.1 ｜ **The Standards for Mathematical Practice**

MP1.   Make sense of problems and persevere in solving them.

MP2.   Reason abstractly and quantitatively.

MP3.   Construct viable arguments and critique the reasoning of others.

MP4.   Model with mathematics.

MP5.   Use appropriate tools strategically.

MP6.   Attend to precision.

MP7.   Look for and make use of structure.

MP8.   Look for and express regularity in repeated reasoning.

In addition to placing an emphasis on mathematics proficiencies that cross all domains, the mathematical practice standards ensure that students focused on skills and processes don't find themselves engaged in rote activities that provide them no deeper sense of how mathematics works as an integrated whole. For example, solving simple equations can legitimately be seen as conducting a set of executable steps. Demonstrating an understanding of the process of reasoning, however, is not so straightforward. The Common Core standards ask that students explain each step in the process of solving an equation and construct an argument to justify a solution method

(HSA-REI.A.1). Students who are able to construct coherent representations of the reasoning process involved in solving equations may achieve a clarity that allows them to see the utility of the process over a wider range of problems.

Please note that, as with the content standards, the mathematical practice standards have official identifiers, which we have shortened in this guide's sample lessons. For example, we abbreviate Mathematical Practice 1, officially "CCSS.Math.Practice.MP1," as "MP1."

Implications of the Standards' Structure on Teaching and Learning

Many traditional high school mathematics standards documents are divided into courses rather than conceptual categories. However, standards within the Common Core's conceptual categories are not intended to be used in isolation or for only a single mathematics course. This means that a high school course may include standards from multiple conceptual areas and that the same standard may appear within more than one course as teachers address different aspects of the standard.

A good example of this kind of cross-course applicability is Standard 11 within Algebra's Reasoning with Equations and Inequalities domain (HSA-REI.D.11). This standard asks students to find the solutions to systems of equations approximately, including cases where one or both of the equations are linear, polynomial, rational, absolute value, exponential, or logarithmic. HSA-REI.D.11 may appear in multiple courses as students are introduced to the general concept and then gain familiarity with different kinds of equations during subsequent high school mathematics coursework.

Recognizing teachers' practical need for a course-based organization of the standards, the developers of the Common Core added an appendix to the standards document titled *Appendix A: Designing High School Mathematics Courses Based on the Common Core State Standards* (CCSSI, 2010d), which we will refer to as "Appendix A" from here forward. Appendix A articulates in great detail how the mathematical standards could be arranged within and across high school mathematics courses. We consulted it frequently as we sought to clarify for ourselves how standards content connects within and between grades. Readers who consult Appendix A, the frameworks from the PARCC assessment consortium (PARCC, 2011), and our own analysis in this guide will identify a myriad of dependencies and connections among the conceptual categories. Teachers can use these connections to support the creation of coherent and cohesive unit and lesson plans that promote a deeper understanding of the intricacy and interconnectedness of mathematical concepts.

As noted, there are six conceptual categories described in high school mathematics: Number and Quantity, Algebra, Functions, Modeling, Geometry, and Statistics and Probability. The mathematical practice standards are also integrated within each of these conceptual categories. All six of these conceptual categories contain content intended to be taught to all students, and Appendix A illustrates how, by integrating the categories, the content can be organized into three years of high school. As a conceptual category, Geometry is a little more self-contained than the first three conceptual categories, looking a bit more like a traditional course than the others. The other five conceptual categories are intended to be integrated into three years of school using the traditional U.S. model.

The combining of Number and Quantity, Functions, and Algebra is probably the more familiar organizational structure to many teachers. In fact, the choice to organize the content addressing those concepts as separate categories may seem unusual to teachers accustomed to a course-based structure. It may also be surprising to see functions appear as a separate category rather than integrated with algebraic equations and expressions, as occurs in many state mathematics standards documents. However, teachers may be even more surprised by the intended integration of the content found in the Statistics and Probability category, some of which is seldom taught in the traditional pathways. The notion of integrating the standards in this category with those in the other conceptual categories may present challenges for teachers. Appendix A, which includes suggested units, can provide help with such challenges.

The Modeling category presents a unique structure. No standards are unique to or organized beneath the conceptual category of Modeling;

instead, standards associated with modeling, which are identified by a star symbol (★), are integrated throughout the other categories. Each of these marked standards is meant to indicate a link between mathematics and "everyday life, work, and decision making" (CCSSI, 2010c, p. 72). The introductory text to the Modeling category in the standards document describes what high school modeling should look like. For example, it includes a detailed description of a basic cycle that all students should follow when solving a modeling problem:

> (1) identifying variables in the situation and selecting those that represent essential features, (2) formulating a model by creating and selecting geometric, graphical, tabular, algebraic, or statistical representations that describe relationships between the variables, (3) analyzing and performing operations on these relationships to draw conclusions, (4) interpreting the results of the mathematics in terms of the original situation, (5) validating the conclusions by comparing them with the situation, and then either improving the model or, if it is acceptable, (6) reporting on the conclusions and the reasoning behind them. Choices, assumptions, and approximations are present throughout this cycle. (pp. 72–73)

This section of the standards document provides some useful insights into modeling, and we urge teachers to read through it carefully. While the modeling standards identified within the other conceptual areas are accompanied by explanations, these explanations are at times terse. The introduction to the Modeling category is the only place that describes the writers' intent in detail, including information on what types of contexts the writers of the Common Core expect students to be working with and what models should look like.

How to Begin Implementation

The standards document and its appendixes do offer some ideas for how to get started planning instruction and teaching the standards, and here in this guide, we share our own best advice.

Focus on the mathematical practice standards

The Standards for Mathematical Practice are found in two places in the standards document: in the introduction and in the overview of each grade. Within the introduction, they are described in a comprehensive fashion, with a small number of examples given for the different grades. The guidance found in the introduction provides further valuable insight into each mathematical practice standard, and we recommend that teachers become extremely familiar with these descriptions and spend some time planning how to incorporate the practices into each course. In the chapters to come, we offer our own ideas about how teachers might integrate the mathematical practice standards with each of the domains in the mathematical content standards.

Focus on critical areas

Within the Standards for Mathematic Content document, each of the conceptual categories includes an introduction to clarify the focus of the standards within that category. In addition, Appendix A groups the standards into "critical areas" for each course on the model course pathways described, and these suggestions can support teachers' efforts to organize the standards into units or coherent blocks.

We believe the way for teachers to promote the development of strong foundational knowledge and deep understanding of the concepts in these courses is to concentrate lessons on four to six critical areas, whether those are the areas identified by Appendix A or areas identified at a local level. Selecting a small number of critical areas for a given school year, and using these as the major focus of the majority of curriculum time, allows teachers to guide students to deeper, richer understanding of mathematical concepts.

Focus on connections

The Common Core mathematics standards are designed to be coherent within and across grades. Appendix A of the standards document can provide ideas on how to organize the standards for coherence within a course, and this guide's chapters on the six conceptual categories (and the domains, clusters, and standards within them) shed light on how the standards connect across grades. We provide this information to underscore that each standard is best understood not as completely new knowledge or skills but as an extension of ideas presented in previous grades. As teachers elicit past understandings, students can begin to build on those understandings, developing a deeper knowledge about a given concept. Identifying the logical progression of mathematical concepts also gives teachers a tool for identifying gaps in understanding or accelerating content, if that is desirable.

* * *

As noted, our intention in this quick-start guide is to provide a sense of the scope of each high school mathematics standard and explain how the standards are related to each other across both grade bands and categories. We also make connections with the Standards for Mathematical Practice for each domain. Please be aware that what we present are only a few examples of such connections, and we do not mean to suggest that no other connections can or should be made. Teachers should build on the information here to strengthen their own practice and enhance their implementation of the Common Core standards.

Now that we've looked at the overall structure of the Common Core standards for high school mathematics, we will examine each conceptual category in turn.

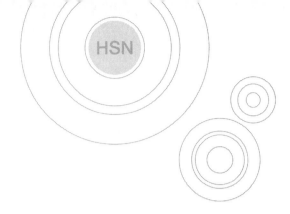

CHAPTER 2

Number and Quantity

The first of the six conceptual categories within the Standards for Mathematical Content is Number and Quantity (HSN), which covers concepts about numbers and number systems, and quantities (numbers with units). These concepts are spread through four domains:

- The Real Number System (HSN-RN)
- Quantities (HSN-Q)
- The Complex Number System (HSN-CN)
- Vector and Matrix Quantities (HSN-VM)

In this chapter, we'll look at each of these domains in turn and examine how the content within the domain connects and builds across the standards.

The Real Number System

The standards document's introduction to the Number and Quantity category makes the point that students have been building their conceptions of numbers and number systems throughout their educational career. The Real Number System is the first of two domains in this category that extends this understanding of number systems.

Students will touch on several mathematical practice standards as they explore the real number system. As they use past knowledge of the properties of numbers to explain new concepts—for example, the meaning of rational exponents—they're constructing an argument using stated assumptions and previously established results, making conjectures about the rational number system, and using examples and counterexamples to make their case. The standards directing that students explain "why" or "how" also require the justification of conclusions, communicating those justifications to others, and responding to the arguments of others. All of these skills are associated with Mathematical Practice Standard 3, "Construct viable arguments and critique the reasoning of others." In addition, as they communicate these arguments and ideas, students will be "attending to precision" as they explain their reasoning (Mathematical Practice Standard 6). Students will also be using Mathematical Practice Standard 7, "Look for and make use of structure," as they analyze specific examples to find patterns and to develop a sense of the overall structure of the real number system.

The Real Number System domain contains three standards, organized into two clusters.

Extend the properties of exponents to rational exponents

Let's take a look at Cluster A within the Real Number System domain (see Figure 2.1).

Figure 2.1　|　**Extend the Properties of Exponents to Rational Exponents**

1. Explain how the definition of the meaning of rational exponents follows from extending the properties of integer exponents to those values, allowing for a notation for radicals in terms of rational exponents. *For example, we define $5^{1/3}$ to be the cube root of 5 because we want $(5^{1/3})^3 = 5^{(1/3)3}$ to hold, so $5^{(1/3)3}$ must equal 5.*
2. Rewrite expressions involving radicals and rational exponents using the properties of exponents.

The concept of exponents (powers of 10) is first introduced in 5th grade and developed further in grades 6–7 as students work with numerical expressions involving exponents. In grade 8, students learn to work with radicals and integer exponents, applying the "properties of integer exponents to generate equivalent expressions" (8.EE.A.1). Here at the high school level, this cluster expands upon the knowledge base developed in those previous grades not only by requiring students to use the properties of exponents to rewrite expressions but also by requiring them to construct an explanation for the properties of rational exponents. This deep understanding will help students connect integer and rational exponents with content covered in other standards, such as the creation, interpretation, and use of exponential expressions and equations addressed in the conceptual category of Algebra (see HSA-SSE.A and HSA-SSE.B, pp. 27–29).

Use properties of rational and irrational numbers

Cluster B in the Real Number System domain (see Figure 2.2) is one of the few in the Common Core that includes just one standard.

HSN-RN.B

Figure 2.2 | **Use Properties of Rational and Irrational Numbers**

3. Explain why the sum or product of two rational numbers is rational; that the sum of a rational number and an irrational number is irrational; and that the product of a nonzero rational number and an irrational number is irrational.

The Common Core mathematics standards are written to build an understanding of the mathematical number systems and develop it throughout the grades, from the introduction of counting numbers in kindergarten to the introduction of irrational numbers in 8th grade. Students are first introduced to the full system of rational numbers in 6th grade, where they develop an understanding of rational numbers as points on a number line (6.NS.C.6–7). In 7th grade, they apply their understanding of rational numbers and operations to perform arithmetic on rational numbers and to solve real-world problems involving rational numbers (7.NS.A). Finally, the concept of irrational numbers is introduced in 8th grade (8.NS.A). This cluster extends that understanding of rational and irrational numbers so that students learn to explain and use the properties of rational and irrational numbers. Understanding these properties allows students to work with rational and irrational numbers found in polynomials (e.g., HSA-APR.D.6) and other equations in Algebra.

Quantities ★

Quantities is one of two domains in the Number and Quantity category that focus on numbers with units. Here, units are looked at as tools for problem solving rather than just as tools for measurement (e.g., centimeters or grams). An ability to work with units will help students tackle real-world problems, including the vector and matrix quantities that are described in the last domain within this conceptual category.

The Quantities domain has a clear relationship to Mathematical Practice Standard 2, as students must be able to contextualize and decontextualize quantities and the meaning of those quantities in given problem situations. In addition, students are using familiar mathematical concepts (units and measurement) to model real-world problems, a focus of Mathematical Practice Standard 4.

The domain consists of three standards in a single cluster.

Reason quantitatively and use units to solve problems

Let's look more closely at the connections between this set of standards (see Figure 2.3) and the content addressed throughout the mathematical content standards.

Figure 2.3 | **Reason Quantitatively and Use Units to Solve Problems**   HSN-Q.A

1. Use units as a way to understand problems and to guide the solution of multi-step problems; choose and interpret units consistently in formulas; choose and interpret the scale and the origin in graphs and data displays.
2. Define appropriate quantities for the purpose of descriptive modeling.
3. Choose a level of accuracy appropriate to limitations on measurement when reporting quantities.

Standard 1 (HSN-Q.A.1) first focuses on unit analysis as a problem-solving technique and an interpretation tool and then connects it to graphing by examining the scale and origin of graphs and data displays. The use of units in problems builds from 1st grade, when students measure and express length as a whole number of length units, to 8th grade, when students choose units of appropriate size for very large or very small quantities. Standard 1 extends those skills, encouraging students to work with units not simply as a conversion task once they've found the answer to a problem but as a way of understanding the problem and guiding solutions, including those in graphs. This view of units provides students with a deeper understanding of the concept and greater flexibility to find solutions to real-world problems. The increased focus on quantities as critical for problem solving connects directly to the conceptual category of Statistics and Probability, as students use data from experiments to compare treatments or evaluate reports based on data (found in the Making Inferences and Justifying Conclusions domain).

Standard 2 (HSN-Q.A.2) may be a bit difficult to decipher, in that the language used is somewhat specialized and the description lacks detail. Thankfully, the introduction to the Number and Quantity conceptual category provides some useful information about this standard's meaning, explaining that students will encounter "novel situations" in which they must "conceive the attributes of interest" (CCSSI, 2010c, p. 58). In other words, when students are faced with a problem situation in which what should be measured is not clear, they must be able to define a measure that will allow them to present their findings. The example given in the introduction illustrates possible measures of overall highway safety (fatalities per year, fatalities per vehicle-mile traveled, etc.). Other examples of problem situations might include determining the best ways to measure the success of "green" initiatives or of a webinar presentation. These problem situations can be evaluated in several different ways, and students can define what quantities they believe will best evaluate a given situation (e.g., cost savings per year or energy reduction per month for the "green" initiative or the number of participants in a webinar). This perspective on quantity will come in handy in the Statistics and Probability category when evaluating treatments in a randomized experiment (HSS-IC.B.5) or reports (HSS-IC.B.6).

Standard 3 (HSN-Q.A.3) describes the use of precision and significant digits when measuring. This standard builds on students' understanding of measurement developed through the grades and helps them solve problems involving measurements, including problems found in Geometry within the Geometric Measurement and Dimension domain.

The Complex Number System

As described in the standards document's introduction to Number and Quantity, there are two domains that focus on number systems. The Real Number System domain focuses on the real number system, extending students' understanding of rational and irrational numbers. The Complex Number System domain addresses the concepts and skills that students will need when working with quadratics. A glance at the domain makes clear that the complex number system is considered advanced content—six of the nine standards are marked with a (+), designating them as content for students who intend to take advanced mathematics courses that are not required of all students. According to Appendix A, the three standards in this domain that are designated for all students are appropriate for upper-level high school mathematics courses, such as Algebra II or Mathematics II.

As students are asked to compute with complex numbers, represent them on the complex plane and calculate the distance and the midpoint between numbers, or use complex numbers in polynomial identities or equations, they will need to draw on prior knowledge such as their understanding of operational properties, the coordinate plane, and how to solve algebraic equations. When students analyze relationships and compare new problems to what they've worked with in the past, they use their prior knowledge to "make sense of problems" (Mathematical Practice Standard 1). Strategically applying the skills, techniques, and technologies they've used with the real number system to complex numbers will facilitate symbolic manipulation as well as expand their set of "tools" for problem solving (Mathematical Practice Standard 5). As students explain why the two forms of a given number are equivalent or show how the Fundamental Theorem of Algebra is true for quadratic polynomials, they are making conjectures, analyzing situations, and communicating their conclusions—skills associated with Mathematical Practice Standard 3, "Construct viable arguments and critique the reasoning of others." The ability to communicate their conclusions precisely, using clear definitions, will be useful when they're asked to explain features of the complex number system.

The domain's nine standards are organized into three clusters.

Perform arithmetic operations with complex numbers

This first cluster (see Figure 2.4) lays the foundation for working with complex numbers by introducing the basic concept of complex numbers ($i^2 = -1$), the form of complex numbers, and basic operations with complex numbers using the commutative, associative, and distributive properties.

HSN-CN.A

Figure 2.4 | **Perform Arithmetic Operations with Complex Numbers**

1. Know there is a complex number i such that $i^2 = -1$, and every complex number has the form $a + bi$ with a and b real.
2. Use the relation $i^2 = -1$ and the commutative, associative, and distributive properties to add, subtract, and multiply complex numbers.
3. (+) Find the conjugate of a complex number; use conjugates to find moduli and quotients of complex numbers.

Understanding these foundations of complex numbers depends heavily on the understanding of the properties of operations and the concepts of number systems that students have developed throughout the grades. The content of the first cluster, which Appendix A identifies as appropriate for Algebra II or Mathematics II courses, prepares students for the second and third clusters of this domain, in which students use their understanding of complex numbers to create graphs and solve polynomial equations and identities.

Represent complex numbers and their operations on the complex plane

All three standards in Cluster B (see Figure 2.5) are marked with a (+), indicating that they are advanced content. Not all students are required to learn these standards, which are not designated for assessment by the assessment consortia.

Figure 2.5 | **Represent Complex Numbers and Their Operations on the Complex Plane**

4. (+) Represent complex numbers on the complex plane in rectangular and polar form (including real and imaginary numbers), and explain why the rectangular and polar forms of a given complex number represent the same number.
5. (+) Represent addition, subtraction, multiplication, and conjugation of complex numbers geometrically on the complex plane; use properties of this representation for computation. *For example, $(-1 + \sqrt{3}i)^3 = 8$ because $(-1 + \sqrt{3}i)$ has modulus 2 and argument* $120°$.
6. (+) Calculate the distance between numbers in the complex plane as the modulus of the difference, and the midpoint of a segment as the average of the numbers at its endpoints.

Requiring students to represent numbers in the complex plane calls on them to use their understanding of the Cartesian coordinate system developed beginning in the 6th grade and their understanding of radian measures as described in the Trigonometric Functions domain of the Functions category (see HSF-TF.A, p. 57). When students calculate the distance between numbers and the midpoint of a segment on the complex plane, they will rely upon on their understanding of distance and midpoints on the Cartesian coordinate system, content found in the Number System and Geometry domains at the middle school level. Understanding how to calculate midpoints on the complex plane, in turn, will help students prepare to continue studies in Calculus and other advanced mathematics courses.

Use complex numbers in polynomial identities and equations

This cluster of standards (see Figure 2.6) links understanding of the complex number system to content found in the Algebra and Functions domains.

HSN-CN.C

Figure 2.6   **Use Complex Numbers in Polynomial Identities and Equations**
7. Solve quadratic equations with real coefficients that have complex solutions.
8. (+) Extend polynomial identities to the complex numbers. *For example, rewrite* $x^2 + 4$ *as* $(x + 2i)(x - 2i)$.
9. (+) Know the Fundamental Theorem of Algebra; show that it is true for quadratic polynomials.

As students solve quadratics that have complex solutions, they will depend heavily upon the understanding they've gained of quadratic equations as well as the ability they've developed to solve equations with real solutions, described in the Algebra domain (e.g., HSA-REI.B.4). Students who successfully "extend polynomial identities to the complex numbers" to solve problems, as described in Standard 8 (HSN-CN.C.8), will have mastered content in the Algebra cluster "Use polynomial identities to solve problems" (HSA-APR.C). The extension of polynomial identities and knowledge of the Fundamental Theorem of Algebra are both expectations for students preparing to take advanced courses in mathematics, as indicated by the (+) found before Standards 7 and 8.

Vector and Matrix Quantities

This is the final domain within the Number and Quantity conceptual category and the second to refer to the concept of quantities. While the Quantities domain focuses on measured quantities and extends students' understandings of units and problem solving, this domain introduces vector quantities, which are generally used to explain science concepts such as velocity, and matrix quantities, which can be used to represent and manipulate data. All standards within this domain are marked with a (+), indicating that vector and matrix quantities are considered advanced topics and mastery will not be required of all students.

The Vector and Matrix Quantities domain has several standards that require students to reason both qualitatively and quantitatively, as both vectors and matrices have clear real-world connections. As students solve problems (such as those involving velocity vectors or payoffs in a game), the ability to contextualize the problem (or think about the problem as an abstract situation) and to decontextualize the situation (or work with the vectors and matrices as mathematical tools) will help them understand and correctly set up and solve the problem.

The 12 standards in this domain are organized into three clusters.

Represent and model with vector quantities

The first standard (HSN-VM.A.1) in this domain and in this cluster (see Figure 2.7) introduces the very basic idea that vectors have both a magnitude and a direction.

Figure 2.7 | **Represent and Model with Vector Quantities**

1. (+) Recognize vector quantities as having both magnitude and direction. Represent vector quantities by directed line segments, and use appropriate symbols for vectors and their magnitudes (e.g., $\boldsymbol{v}$, $|\boldsymbol{v}|$, $\|\boldsymbol{v}\|$, v).
2. (+) Find the components of a vector by subtracting the coordinates of an initial point from the coordinates of a terminal point.
3. (+) Solve problems involving velocity and other quantities that can be represented by vectors.

Students should be familiar with the general idea that "some quantities need both size and direction to be described" (National Research Council, Committee on a Conceptual Framework for New K–12 Science Education Standards, 2012, p. 115), as this concept is commonly found in elementary school science standards. In later grades, the idea that lines can be described with an angle and a measure is developed when students study radian measures (found in HSF-TF.A).

Standard 2 (HSN-VM.A.2) necessarily builds on Standard 1 as students perform operations on vectors. Standard 3 (HSN-VM.A.3) asks students to apply the conceptual understandings developed by Standards 1 and 2, focusing on the application of vectors to physical quantities. This idea can easily be integrated with a physical science unit as students begin to study Newton's laws of motion.

Perform operations on vectors

Cluster B within the Vector and Matrix Quantities domain (see Figure 2.8) builds upon the introduction to vectors found in Cluster A. As students develop their understanding of vectors by adding, subtracting, multiplying, and dividing them, they'll also touch on basic skills and understanding found in the Geometry conceptual category, such as making geometric constructions (from the Congruence domain) and scaling geometric figures (from the Similarity, Right Triangles, and Trigonometry domain). These skills will help students prepare for upper-level mathematics courses such as Calculus.

HSN-VM.B

Figure 2.8 | **Perform Operations on Vectors**

4. (+) Add and subtract vectors.
  a. Add vectors end-to-end, component-wise, and by the parallelogram rule. Understand that the magnitude of a sum of two vectors is typically not the sum of the magnitudes.
  b. Given two vectors in magnitude and direction form, determine the magnitude and direction of their sum.
  c. Understand vector subtraction $v - w$ as $v + (-w)$, where $-w$ is the additive inverse of w, with the same magnitude as w and pointing in the opposite direction. Represent vector subtraction graphically by connecting the tips in the appropriate order, and perform vector subtraction component-wise.
5. (+) Multiply a vector by a scalar.
  a. Represent scalar multiplication graphically by scaling vectors and possibly reversing their direction; perform scalar multiplication component-wise, e.g., as $c(v_x, v_y) = (cv_x, cv_y)$.
  b. Compute the magnitude of a scalar multiple cv using $\|cv\| = |c|v$. Compute the direction of cv knowing that when $|c|v \neq 0$, the direction of cv is either along v (for $c > 0$) or against v (for $c < 0$).

Perform operations on matrices and use matrices in applications

Students begin working with simple systems of equations in 8th grade, and their skills in solving systems of equations are further extended through standards in the Reasoning with Equations and Inequalities domain of the

Algebra category. While solving systems of equations is required of all students, representing systems of equations as matrices (content found within HSA-REI.C.8–9) is marked with a (+) and therefore not required of all students. This is further confirmed in Appendix A of the standards document, where all content regarding matrices is found in the fourth-year course. The combined content on matrices from both the Number and Quantity and the Algebra categories provides a holistic view of matrices, allowing students to work more fluently with them.

The content found in Algebra sheds light on what matrices represent in algebraic terms. This final cluster within the Vector and Matrix Quantities domain focuses on matrices as ways to represent and manipulate data and as mathematical entities that can be added, subtracted, and multiplied (see Figure 2.9). Students can then use their skills with matrices to multiply a vector, connecting the concepts found in this domain with those in the Algebra category's Reasoning with Equations and Inequalities domain. Again, this content is meant to prepare students for upper-level courses such as Calculus and Physics.

Figure 2.9 | **Perform Operations on Matrices and Use Matrices in Applications**   HSN-VM.C

   6. (+) Use matrices to represent and manipulate data, e.g., to represent payoffs or incidence relationships in a network.
   7. (+) Multiply matrices by scalars to produce new matrices, e.g., as when all of the payoffs in a game are doubled.
   8. (+) Add, subtract, and multiply matrices of appropriate dimensions.
   9. (+) Understand that, unlike multiplication of numbers, matrix multiplication for square matrices is not a commutative operation, but still satisfies the associative and distributive properties.
  10. (+) Understand that the zero and identity matrices play a role in matrix addition and multiplication similar to the role of 0 and 1 in the real numbers. The determinant of a square matrix is nonzero if and only if the matrix has a multiplicative inverse.
  11. (+) Multiply a vector (regarded as a matrix with one column) by a matrix of suitable dimensions to produce another vector. Work with matrices as transformations of vectors.
  12. (+) Work with 2 × 2 matrices as transformations of the plane, and interpret the absolute value of the determinant in terms of area.

CHAPTER 3

Algebra

In this chapter, we'll examine the high school mathematics standards in the conceptual category of Algebra, again discussing the content by domain. For each domain, we will first give an overview of how the domain relates to the other domains in Algebra and how the contents of the domain relate to the Standards for Mathematical Practice. We will then look at each cluster within the domain, identifying the connections among each cluster's content and describing how the content differs and builds across grades and conceptual areas. This close analysis is aimed at clarifying the meaning and developmental progression of each standard within the context of the entirety of the Common Core standards for mathematics.

The Algebra category (HSA) is subdivided into the following domains:

- Seeing Structure in Expressions (HSA-SSE)
- Arithmetic with Polynomials and Rational Expressions (HSA-APR)
- Creating Equations (HSA-CED)
- Reasoning with Equations and Inequalities (HSA-REI)

Taken together, these domains are designed to help students understand, create, and manipulate expressions, equations, and inequalities. The first two domains focus on expressions; the last two, on equations and inequalities.

Seeing Structure in Expressions

The Seeing Structure in Expressions domain provides a foundation for understanding the structure and use of expressions, which students will continue to develop throughout their study of algebra. Whether students are interpreting the structure of expressions or writing expressions in equivalent forms to solve problems, they'll benefit from the ability to shift perspective on a mathematical problem. When asked to choose which equivalent form would best reveal the properties of the quantity involved, students must engage in a process that requires both thinking about the problem's context (e.g., finding an approximate equivalent monthly interest rate) and thinking about the expression in terms of the numbers and variables that need to be manipulated. This ability to shift perspective in order to create a structure for a new problem is reasoning "abstractly and quantitatively"—a skill identified in Mathematical Practice Standard 2. In addition, the ★ appended to standards found in both Seeing Structure in Expressions clusters identifies them as modeling standards and thus directly related to Mathematical Practice Standard 4, "Model with mathematics," in which students should have the opportunity to apply the mathematics that they know to real-world problems.

In the second cluster, students must derive the formula for the sum of a finite geometric series, using their ability to notice regularity (patterns) while expanding terms in order to generalize to a formula. This ability applies to Mathematical Practice Standard 8, which requires students to "look for and express regularity in repeated reasoning."

Having looked at the domain as a whole, we will now take a closer look at its four standards, which are grouped in two clusters.

Interpret the structure of expressions

In 7th grade, students begin performing algebraic manipulations with the goal of rewriting an expression into different forms so that they "can shed light on the problem and how quantities in it are related" (7.EE.A.2). In addition, students use equations to solve problems, constructing equations of specific types and "reasoning about the quantities" (7.EE.B.4). These skills continue to build in 8th grade, where students move on to solving linear equations and simultaneous pairs of linear equations (8.EE.C.7–8). By high school, then, students should be comfortable with simple algebraic manipulations and have a broad understanding of how to use algebraic equations in the context of problem situations, which is the focus of Cluster A (see Figure 3.1).

HSA-SSE.A

Figure 3.1 | **Interpret the Structure of Expressions**

1. Interpret expressions that represent a quantity in terms of its context. ★
  a. Interpret parts of an expression, such as terms, factors, and coefficients.
  b. Interpret complicated expressions by viewing one or more of their parts as a single entity. *For example, interpret $P(1 + r)^n$ as the product of P and a factor not depending on P.*
2. Use the structure of an expression to identify ways to rewrite it. *For example, see $x^4 - y^4$ as $(x^2)^2 - (y^2)^2$, thus recognizing it as a difference of squares that can be factored as $(x^2 - y^2)(x^2 + y^2)$.*

This cluster's blend of skills (algebraic manipulation and the creation of algebraic equations) helps develop students' ability to shift their perspective on algebraic expressions, thinking about the parts of an expression both as separate pieces and as an entire expression. An analogy might be found in the language arts, when students are able to view phrases and words as parts, such as subjects or prepositional phrases, while still being able to grasp the meaning of the sentence as a whole. When students can shift perspective in this manner, they are able to simplify and rewrite expressions by "chunking" parts of more complicated expressions either to make them easier to work with or to reveal a different aspect of the expression's meaning. These skills build upon understanding developed in earlier grades about algebraic manipulation that requires judgment (mindfulness about reasoning) and fluency, and they help students develop the ability to write expressions in equivalent forms in order to solve problems, which is the object of the next cluster in this domain.

Write expressions in equivalent forms to solve problems

The standards in Cluster B of Seeing Structure in Expressions (see Figure 3.2) have their immediate roots in the student's ability to "use the structure of an expression to identify ways to rewrite it" (HSA-SSE.A.2).

Figure 3.2 | Write Expressions in Equivalent Forms to Solve Problems

3. Choose and produce an equivalent form of an expression to reveal and explain properties of the quantity represented by the expression. ★
   a. Factor a quadratic expression to reveal the zeros of the function it defines.
   b. Complete the square in a quadratic expression to reveal the maximum or minimum value of the function it defines.
   c. Use the properties of exponents to transform expressions for exponential functions. *For example, the expression* 1.15^t *can be rewritten as* $(1.15^{1/2})^{12t} \approx 1.012^{12t}$ *to reveal the approximate equivalent monthly interest rate if the annual rate is 15%.*
4. Derive the formula for the sum of a finite geometric series (when the common ratio is not 1), and use the formula to solve problems. *For example, calculate mortgage payments.* ★

Once students have learned ways to rewrite an expression, they can choose forms of expressions and explain their properties, demonstrating their mathematical reasoning and communication skills. The other skills found within this cluster, including factoring a quadratic expression, completing the square of a quadratic expression, and transforming expressions for exponential functions, have their basis in middle school standards and are natural extensions of the skills needed to factor and rewrite linear expressions (7.EE.A, 7.EE.B, 8.EE.C) and work with exponents (8.EE.A, HSN-RN.A). Students will build on these understandings in Algebra II as they work more with sequences and series. Standard 4 (HSA-SSE.B.4), which Appendix A places in Algebra II (or Mathematics III), can be used in these courses in conjunction with HSF-BF.A.2 in the Functions category.

Arithmetic with Polynomials and Rational Expressions

Students learn to perform computations throughout the grades. In 1st and 2nd grades, they're introduced to the concept of unknowns in equations involving addition and subtraction. Students build upon this skill in grades 3 through 5 as they add multiplication and division to their repertoire and begin to work with whole numbers and integers. In grade 6, students apply those foundational understandings about computation and variables to simple algebraic expressions (6.EE.A.1–4). These skills are further developed throughout middle school as students work with real-world problems, manipulate equations, and add the concept of rational numbers to their knowledge set.

Mastery of the content in the Arithmetic with Polynomials and Rational Expressions domain's four clusters depends heavily on the understandings built across prior grades and on mastery of content found in the "Interpret the structure of expressions" cluster in the Seeing Structure in Expressions domain. There is also a clear connection between computing with polynomial and rational expressions and reasoning with polynomial and rational functions, content found in the Reasoning with Equations and Inequalities domain in the Algebra category, the Interpreting Functions domain in Functions, and the Complex Number System domain in Number and Quantity.

In addition to these connections, the standards in this domain are linked to several mathematical practice standards. Being able to make connections from previous understandings to the newer concept of polynomials reflects Mathematical Practice Standards 1 and 7, making sense of problems (by considering analogous problems) and looking for and making use of structure (being able to shift perspective to view the polynomials as single objects or as being composed of several objects). As students use algebraic skills to solve problems, they're making sense of quantities and their relationships in problem-solving situations, a skill related to Mathematical Practice Standard 2 ("Reason abstractly and quantitatively"). The ability to explain steps in problem solving, or to develop mathematical proofs such as proofs of polynomial identities, is directly related to constructing viable arguments (Mathematical Practice Standard 3) and communicating precisely to others (Mathematical Practice Standard 6). Finally, as the introduction to the Algebra conceptual category makes clear, technology can be used to "experiment with algebraic expressions, perform complicated algebraic manipulations, and understand how algebraic manipulations behave" (CCSSI, 2010c, p. 62)—thereby using appropriate tools strategically (Mathematical Practice Standard 5).

Now that we've looked at the domain as a whole, we'll take a closer look at its seven standards organized into four clusters.

Perform arithmetic operations on polynomials

Cluster A (see Figure 3.3) of the Arithmetic with Polynomials and Rational Expressions domain is another of the few that contain just one standard.

Figure 3.3   **Perform Arithmetic Operations on Polynomials**
1. Understand that polynomials form a system analogous to the integers, namely, they are closed under the operations of addition, subtraction, and multiplication; add, subtract, and multiply polynomials.

Standard 1 (HSA-APR.A.1) is clearly and explicitly connected to an understanding of the system of integers, which has its roots in the number system standards in grade 6. While the concept of number systems forming closed sets under given operations is not formally introduced prior to this standard, students have been using the properties of integers in their earlier work with expressions. This basic understanding of integer properties will help students as they learn to add, subtract, and multiply polynomials. As polynomials (and integers) are not closed under division, division of polynomials is addressed in Standard 6 (HSA-APR.D.6) of this domain, which we'll look at shortly.

Understand the relationship between zeros and factors of polynomials

Cluster B (see Figure 3.4) may seem oddly placed within the structure of the Algebra category. To anyone approaching the standards in the order presented within the standards document rather than as they are addressed in

Figure 3.4 | **Understand the Relationship Between Zeros and Factors of Polynomials**

2. Know and apply the Remainder Theorem: For a polynomial $p(x)$ and a number a, the remainder on division by $x - a$ is $p(a)$, so $p(a) = 0$ if and only if $(x - a)$ is a factor of $p(x)$.
3. Identify zeros of polynomials when suitable factorizations are available, and use the zeros to construct a rough graph of the function defined by the polynomial.

the Appendix A courses, it can be confusing to see the Remainder Theorem, addressed in Standard 2 (HSA-APR.B.2) introduced before division with polynomials. A closer look clarifies that the Remainder Theorem is included here to introduce one method of determining the solution for the zeros of a given polynomial.

Standard 3 (HSA-APR.B.3) can be divided into two parts: identifying the zeros of a polynomial and using those zeros to create a rough graph of the polynomial expression. The first half, identification of zeros, has its roots in the ability to manipulate and perform arithmetic operations on expressions (HSA-APR.A.1, HSA-SSE.A, HSA-SSE.B.3). Appendix A makes it clear that the ability to work with linear and quadratic equations should be developed first; working with polynomials is recommended for upper-level courses. The second half of the standard, which addresses using zeros to create a graph, builds upon the graphing skills students begin to develop in 6th grade and cultivate throughout middle school. By 8th grade, they're able to graph systems of linear equations to solve problems and compare functions represented graphically. Standard 3 logically follows from those foundations, as students sketch rough graphs of a polynomial. This skill is further extended in standards found in the Algebra category's fourth domain (HSA-REI.D; see p. 40).

Use polynomial identities to solve problems

Cluster C (see Figure 3.5) in this domain builds on students' understanding of polynomials, which is developed in Clusters A and B.

The ability to prove mathematical concepts is rooted in learning that begins in 1st grade, when the standards call on students to explain their

---

Figure 3.5 | **Use Polynomial Identities to Solve Problems**

HSA-APR.C

4. Prove polynomial identities and use them to describe numerical relationships. *For example, the polynomial identity* $(x^2 + y^2)^2 = (x^2 - y^2)^2 + (2xy)^2$ *can be used to generate Pythagorean triples.*

5. (+) Know and apply the Binomial Theorem for the expansion of $(x + y)^n$ in powers of x and y for a positive integer n, where x and y are any numbers, with coefficients determined for example by Pascal's Triangle.*

* The Binomial Theorem can be proved by mathematical induction or by a combinatorial argument.

---

reasoning when implementing a given strategy, and continues through 8th grade, when students must explain a proof. While explaining strategies, methods, and patterns found in mathematics is emphasized throughout the grades, students are not expected to *develop* their own proof prior to high school. That this cluster is designed to be taught after students have been introduced to proofs in Geometry is evidenced by its placement in the Algebra II course in Appendix A, the example content related to polynomials, and the advanced nature of Standard 5 (HSA-APR.C.5), indicated by the (+).

Rewrite rational expressions

The final cluster in the domain deepens student understandings of arithmetic with expressions to include rational expressions (see Figure 3.6).

Figure 3.6 | **Rewrite Rational Expressions**

HSA-APR.D

6. Rewrite simple rational expressions in different forms; write $a(x)/b(x)$ in the form $q(x) + r(x)/b(x)$, where $a(x)$, $b(x)$, $q(x)$, and $r(x)$ are polynomials with the degree of $r(x)$ less than the degree of $b(x)$, using inspection, long division, or, for the more complicated examples, a computer algebra system.

7. (+) Understand that rational expressions form a system analogous to the rational numbers, closed under addition, subtraction, multiplication, and division by a non-zero rational expression; add, subtract, multiply, and divide rational expressions.

Students are first introduced to the system of rational numbers in 6th grade, when they "apply and extend previous understandings of numbers to the system of rational numbers" (6.NS.C.5–8). In 7th grade, we see a developing understanding of operations with rational numbers that serves as the foundation for understanding that rational numbers are closed under the basic operations. This cluster also builds on an understanding of operations on polynomials (HSA-APR.A.1) and an ability to understand and manipulate expressions (HSA-SSE.A, HSA-SSE.B). These skills are considered advanced skills; Standard 6 (HSA-APR.D.6) is typically found in Algebra II, and Standard 7 (HSA-APR.D.7) is designated with a (+), indicating that it is considered advanced content.

Creating Equations ★

With this domain, the Algebra category's standards move from focusing on expressions to focusing on equations. Creating Equations specifically deals with the *creation* of equations and inequalities (the fourth and final Algebra domain focuses on *reasoning* with equations and inequalities). Students have been working with equations and inequalities to solve problems since the 6th grade, when they are first asked to solve real-world problems using equations and inequalities in specific forms (6.EE.B.7–8, 6.EE.C.9). By 8th grade, students are asked to solve real-world problems involving two linear equations in two variables (8.EE.C.8). But knowing how to solve real-world problems is only part of the foundational skills required to create equations. Appendix A specifies that students' understanding of quantities (numbers with units) and how to work with them, as described in the conceptual category Number and Quantity, is essential for knowing how to create equations from problem situations, formulating quadratic equations and simple rational and exponential equations.

As indicated by the ★ beside the domain heading, all standards within Creating Equations are also considered modeling standards, resulting in an obvious connection to Mathematical Practice Standard 4, "Model with mathematics." More specifically, we can see that students will use familiar mathematical concepts and skills (e.g., understanding of the structure of equations and inequalities and algebraic manipulation) to model problem situations. Whether they are solving problems by creating equations, interpreting solutions to equations or inequalities in a modeling context, or rearranging formulas to highlight quantities of interest, this domain involves students in both quantitative and qualitative reasoning, work associated with Mathematical Practice Standard 2. A less obvious connection, but one still easily inferred from the standards in this domain, is to Mathematical Practice Standard 5, "Use appropriate tools strategically," since the standards readily lend themselves to the use of technology while students graph equations and represent solutions.

This domain contains four standards in just one cluster.

Create equations that describe numbers or relationships

Creating equations in problem-solving situations is a skill with roots in middle school mathematics, where students are introduced to solving problems that require the construction of simple equations and inequalities. The standards in this cluster (see Figure 3.7) build upon that ability as students start to work with linear and quadratic functions, simple rational and exponential functions, equations with two or more variables, problems with constraints, and formulas that need to be rearranged.

Figure 3.7 | **Create Equations That Describe Numbers or Relationships**

1. Create equations and inequalities in one variable and use them to solve problems. *Include equations arising from linear and quadratic functions, and simple rational and exponential functions.*
2. Create equations in two or more variables to represent relationships between quantities; graph equations on coordinate axes with labels and scales.
3. Represent constraints by equations or inequalities, and by systems of equations and/or inequalities, and interpret solutions as viable or nonviable options in a modeling context. *For example, represent inequalities describing nutritional and cost constraints on combinations of different foods.*
4. Rearrange formulas to highlight a quantity of interest, using the same reasoning as in solving equations. *For example, rearrange Ohm's law V = IR to highlight resistance R.*

The content described in Standards 1–4 (HSA-CED.A.1–4) connects readily to the content in the next domain, Reasoning with Equations and Inequalities, because the ability to reason with equations and inequalities is necessary for the successful creation and use of equations for problem solving. Many of the skills associated with creating equations and using them to solve problems are required beyond the Algebra category, in particular when students build and reason with functions.

Reasoning with Equations and Inequalities

The fourth and final Algebra domain addresses students' ability to solve and reason with equations and systems of equations. Per the sequence of the Common Core mathematics standards, this is an ability students developed in several earlier grades, particularly in middle school, and this prior learning will be applied as students work with and communicate about more complex equations and inequalities. In high school, a unit about reasoning with equations can easily be developed by combining this domain with the first Algebra domain (Seeing Structure in Expressions), because the emphases are similar.

As the domain name suggests, students' reasoning with equations and inequalities depends heavily upon their application of Mathematical Practice Standard 2 ("Reason abstractly and quantitatively") as they develop justifications for their solution methods and construct a proof. Two additional mathematical practice standards, on the development of viable arguments (Mathematical Practice Standard 3) and attending to precision (Mathematical Practice Standard 6), are also important for students as they construct a formal argument and a proof, both of which require a logical chain of reasoning using clear and precise mathematical language and detail. Mathematical Practice Standard 4, "Model with mathematics," is clearly related to HSA-REI.D.11, which is marked with a ★. Under this standard, students apply what they know about equations and inequalities and graphing to explain why the x-coordinates of the points of intersection of two equations are solutions to the equation, and find the solutions approximately. The Modeling standard indicates an opportunity to help students see how mathematics is part of everyday life. Therefore, while the wording of the standard does not specify that the equations $y = f(x)$ and $y = g(x)$ should be derived from contextual problems, the identifying ★ suggests that they should. Finally, students will strategically use appropriate tools (Mathematical Practice Standard 5) as they represent and solve equations and inequalities using technology such as graphing calculators or computer software.

The Reasoning with Equations and Inequalities domain has 12 standards, which are organized into four clusters.

Understand solving equations as a process of reasoning and explain the reasoning

Many sets of mathematical standards don't recognize the reasoning that students must engage in when solving even simple equations. By contrast, standards within this cluster (see Figure 3.8) take care to emphasize that students are not simply solving equations but are also justifying their solution method using a mathematical argument.

HSA-REI.A

Figure 3.8 | **Understand Solving Equations as a Process of Reasoning and Explain the Reasoning**

1. Explain each step in solving a simple equation as following from the equality of numbers asserted at the previous step, starting from the assumption that the original equation has a solution. Construct a viable argument to justify a solution method.
2. Solve simple rational and radical equations in one variable, and give examples showing how extraneous solutions may arise.

Cluster A's emphasis on expressing the reasoning process is not unusual in the Common Core mathematics standards. From the 1st grade on, the standards explicitly require students to be able to explain both the mathematical concepts that they're learning and their thought processes as they reason about mathematical concepts and problem situations. The use of argument is included in several other places in the high school content standards, including as a possible method of proving theorems (HSA-APR.C.5) or explaining formulas (HSG-GMD.A.1–2; see p. 78).

While Standard 1 (HSA-REI.A.1) involves solving simple equations, Standard 2 (HSA-REI.A.2) moves on to solving rational and radical equations with possible extraneous solutions. Although the second standard does not explicitly state that students should attend to the reasoning process while solving rational and radical equations, its placement within this cluster indicates a focus on the reasoning process. This means that Standard 2 is designed to expand on the ability to reason about solution methods addressed in Standard 1. Indeed, from Appendix A, we know that HSA-REI.A.1 is intended to be taught in a first-year course, while HSA-REI.A.2 is intended for a third-year course. Although both standards are located in the same cluster, they are intended to be taught at very different points in a student's mathematical career.

Solve equations and inequalities in one variable

The standards within Cluster B of the Reasoning with Equations and Inequalities domain (see Figure 3.9) provide students with the opportunity to apply what they've learned about reasoning with algebraic equations.

HSA-REI.B

Figure 3.9	**Solve Equations and Inequalities in One Variable**

3. Solve linear equations and inequalities in one variable, including equations with coefficients represented by letters.
4. Solve quadratic equations in one variable.
  a. Use the method of completing the square to transform any quadratic equation in x into an equation of the form $(x - p)^2 = q$ that has the same solutions. Derive the quadratic formula from this form.
  b. Solve quadratic equations by inspection (e.g., for $x^2 = 49$), taking square roots, completing the square, the quadratic formula and factoring, as appropriate to the initial form of the equation. Recognize when the quadratic formula gives complex solutions and write them as $a \pm bi$ for real numbers a and b.

The skill of solving linear equations and inequalities in one variable can be traced back through the grades, beginning with determining the unknown number in lower elementary school and continuing through solving familiar equations and inequalities in middle school. The standards in this cluster draw upon these earlier foundations to help students begin solving and transforming quadratic equations. In the high school standards, the ability to solve and transform quadratic equations is addressed not only throughout the Algebra category but also in several other categories and domains, including the Complex Number System in Number and Quantity (HSN-CN.C); Linear, Quadratic, and Exponential Models in Functions (HSF-LE.A.3); and Interpreting Categorical and Quantitative Data in Statistics and Probability (HSS-ID.B.6). The Expressing Geometric Properties with Equations domain in Geometry also includes a standard requiring students to solve and transform quadratic equations as they complete the square when working with the equation of a circle (HSG-GPE.A.1).

Solve systems of equations

While Cluster B focuses on single equations, Cluster C in this domain addresses systems of equations (see Figure 3.10). Appendix A makes it clear that the first three standards in this cluster are designed to be taught in the first years of high school math (Algebra I or Integrated Mathematics I and II), while the last two standards, marked with a (+), are associated with advanced coursework.

HSA-REI.C

Figure 3.10 | **Solve Systems of Equations**

5. Prove that, given a system of two equations in two variables, replacing one equation by the sum of that equation and a multiple of the other produces a system with the same solutions.
6. Solve systems of linear equations exactly and approximately (e.g., with graphs), focusing on pairs of linear equations in two variables.
7. Solve a simple system consisting of a linear equation and a quadratic equation in two variables algebraically and graphically. *For example, find the points of intersection between the line $y = -3x$ and the circle $x^2 + y^2 = 3$.*
8. (+) Represent a system of linear equations as a single matrix equation in a vector variable.
9. (+) Find the inverse of a matrix if it exists and use it to solve systems of linear equations (using technology for matrices of dimension 3×3 or greater).

Students are introduced to systems of equations in 8th grade, when they "analyze and solve pairs of simultaneous linear equations" (8.EE.C.8). Standards 5, 6, and 7 in this cluster (HSA-REI.C.5–7) require high school students to attend to their reasoning as they develop a proof about systems of equations and to solve systems consisting of linear equations and a linear equation and a quadratic equation. This newly developed skill is also closely related to skills that students are mastering in Geometry, as they work with intersections and parallel lines (HSG-GPE.B.5).

Standards 8 and 9 (HSA-REI.C.8–9) are a logical extension of the idea of systems of equations, namely, matrices. This content is marked with a (+), indicating that it is considered mathematical content that students should know in order to take advanced courses. If students continue on to the fourth course, they will be working with matrices and vector quantities, and the skills found in these two standards (being able to represent a system of equations in a matrix and being able to find the inverse of a matrix) will be useful as they use matrices in applications.

Represent and solve equations and inequalities graphically

The last cluster found in this domain addresses students' graphing skills in conjunction with algebraic concepts (see Figure 3.11).

HSA-REI.D

Figure 3.11 | **Represent and Solve Equations and Inequalities Graphically**

10. Understand that the graph of an equation in two variables is the set of all its solutions plotted in the coordinate plane, often forming a curve (which could be a line).
11. Explain why the x-coordinates of the points where the graphs of the equations $y = f(x)$ and $y = g(x)$ intersect are the solutions of the equation $f(x) = g(x)$; find the solutions approximately, e.g., using technology to graph the functions, make tables of values, or find successive approximations. Include cases where $f(x)$ and/or $g(x)$ are linear, polynomial, rational, absolute value, exponential, and logarithmic functions. ★
12. Graph the solutions to a linear inequality in two variables as a half-plane (excluding the boundary in the case of a strict inequality), and graph the solution set to a system of linear inequalities in two variables as the intersection of the corresponding half-planes.

The ability to graph on the coordinate plane has its roots in 5th grade Geometry (5.G.A). In 6th grade, students begin to relate variables found in equations to graphs (6.EE.C.9), and by 8th grade, they're introduced to graphing pairs of simultaneous linear equations to estimate their solution (8.EE.C.8). The content in this cluster builds on that previous knowledge, extending student understanding of *what* the graph of an equation represents and *why* the x-coordinates of the intersections of the two graphs of the equations $y = f(x)$ and $y = g(x)$ are the solutions to the equation $f(x) = g(x)$. The connection between curves and equations may also assist students as they begin to apply algebraic concepts to geometry (PARCC, 2011). As seen in Appendix A of the standards document, the progression of ideas should begin with linear and exponential equations and inequalities in Algebra I (or Integrated Mathematics I), while the polynomial, rational, radical, absolute value, and exponential functions should be combined in Algebra II (or Mathematics III). As discussed in the PARCC frameworks document, students require a deep understanding of what the graph of an equation in two variables represents before they can successfully graph linear and quadratic functions. Thus, there is a clear connection between this cluster and the conceptual category of Functions, which will be described in the next chapter.

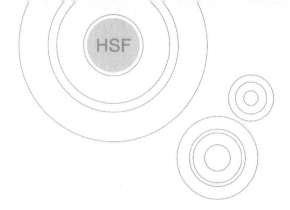

CHAPTER 4

Functions

The third conceptual category in high school mathematics is Functions (HSF). It is divided into four domains:

- Interpreting Functions (HSF-IF)
- Building Functions (HSF-BF)
- Linear, Quadratic, and Exponential Models (HSF-LE)
- Trigonometric Functions (HSF-TF)

This division establishes a logical flow: Students are introduced to the concept of functions and function notation and learn to interpret functions. Then they begin to model relationships by building functions before expanding upon those skills to construct and compare linear, quadratic, and exponential models. Finally, they extend their understanding of functions to trigonometric functions.

Interpreting Functions

The Interpreting Functions domain focuses on building a foundational understanding of functions, including sequences. Students review what functions are, what they look like, and how to interpret them regardless of their representation. As students begin to make sense of functions, in part by explaining the correspondences between the different forms of functions and looking for trends, they may participate in activities that address an important aspect of Mathematical Practice Standard 1, "Make sense of problems and persevere in solving them." After students gain some familiarity with functions, they're expected to use them in the context of problem solving. The ability to understand and represent a problem both in function notation and in a problem context is evidence that students are reasoning abstractly and quantitatively (Mathematical Practice Standard 2) as well as modeling with mathematics (Mathematical Practice Standard 4). When they work to solve problems, students look for and make use of structure (Mathematical Practice Standard 7) as they begin to see a function both as a combination of parts and as a whole entity.

The Interpreting Functions domain has eight standards, organized into three clusters.

Understand the concept of a function and use function notation

Cluster A of this domain (see Figure 4.1) contains standards that build on a baseline understanding of functions, first developed in the 8th grade

Figure 4.1 | Understand the Concept of a Function and Use Function Notation   HSF-IF.A

1. Understand that a function from one set (called the domain) to another set (called the range) assigns to each element of the domain exactly one element of the range. If f is a function and x is an element of its domain, then $f(x)$ denotes the output of f corresponding to the input x. The graph of f is the graph of the equation $y = f(x)$.

2. Use function notation, evaluate functions for inputs in their domains, and interpret statements that use function notation in terms of a context.

3. Recognize that sequences are functions, sometimes defined recursively, whose domain is a subset of the integers. *For example, the Fibonacci sequence is defined recursively by $f(0) = f(1) = 1$, $f(n +1) = f(n) + f(n - 1)$ for $n \geq 1$.*

(8.F.A.1–3). In that cluster, 8th grade students learn to understand functions as a rule, compare properties of functions presented in different ways, and recognize linear functions. In the high school cluster, students come to understand a function as having a domain and range, learn how to evaluate functions for inputs in their domains, and use function notation. Students' familiarity with algebraic concepts and graphing, which has been developed from 6th grade on, will help them learn to work with these new concepts.

After students begin to understand these new aspects of a function, they should be able to connect the concept of a function with sequences, recognizing that sequences are, in fact, functions. This understanding will help them to write and construct arithmetic and geometric sequences, as described in standards in the Building Functions and the Linear, Quadratic, and Exponential Models domains. Students aren't expected to master all aspects of sequences in a single yearlong course, however. As explained in the PARCC frameworks document, "there are a number of individual content standards that specify enduring understandings or recurrent themes" (PARCC, 2011, p. 42). Standard 3 within this domain (HSF-IF.A.3), along with other standards related to sequences in the Building Functions and the Linear, Quadratic, and Exponential Models domains, is highlighted in the PARCC document as an example of how these "recurrent themes" could be stretched across courses. The writers explain that in year one of high school mathematics (Algebra I or Mathematics I), students "talk about sequences as functions," and suggest that the "domain for exponential functions be constrained to the integers," as rational integers may not have been introduced in first-year mathematics courses (p. 47). Students go on to build on these concepts in their third year of mathematics (Algebra II or Mathematics 3), when they become more "formal" in their communication about sequences, and begin to "consider the equality of functions" as it relates to sequences. At this level, students begin to work with extended and restricted domains and can recognize arithmetic and geometric sequences. This work with sequences will also help students as they learn to derive the formula for the sum of a finite geometric series, as found in HSA-SSE.B.4. (see p. 29)

Interpret functions that arise in applications in terms of the context

Cluster B of this domain describes how students will interpret relationships using the concept of functions and function notation (see Figure 4.2).

Figure 4.2 | **Interpret Functions That Arise in Applications in Terms of the Context**   **HSF-IF.B**

4. For a function that models a relationship between two quantities, interpret key features of graphs and tables in terms of the quantities, and sketch graphs showing key features given a verbal description of the relationship. *Key features include: intercepts; intervals where the function is increasing, decreasing, positive, or negative; relative maximums and minimums; symmetries; end behavior; and periodicity.* ★

5. Relate the domain of a function to its graph and, where applicable, to the quantitative relationship it describes. *For example, if the function h(n) gives the number of person-hours it takes to assemble n engines in a factory, then the positive integers would be an appropriate domain for the function.* ★

6. Calculate and interpret the average rate of change of a function (presented symbolically or as a table) over a specified interval. Estimate the rate of change from a graph. ★

While the first cluster of Interpreting Functions focused on understanding the basic concept of a function, this cluster centers on using that understanding while modeling functions in specific contexts. Standards 4, 5, and 6 (HSF-IF.B.4–6) ask students to relate the concepts and terminology introduced in the first cluster to more abstract problem situations. Although the clearest reference to modeling within the text refers to a function that "models a relationship between two quantities," the ★ symbol after each of this cluster's standards indicates that they are considered modeling standards; as such, they are meant to model "quantities and their relationships in physical, economic, public policy, social, and everyday situations" (CCSSI, 2010c, p. 72). This designation provides important information about the *types* of contexts the writers of the Common Core intended students to work with when they are interpreting functions "in terms of the context."

The three standards in Cluster B highlight the three main aspects of interpreting a function: interpreting the key features of graphs and tables in terms of the quantities, relating the domain to both its graph and its context, and calculating and interpreting its average rate of change.

For an example of an Algebra I or Mathematics I lesson addressing HSF-IF.B.4 (in this cluster) and HSF-IF.C.7 (in the next cluster), see **Sample Lesson 1**.

The skill of interpreting graphs has its roots in 5th grade, when students first learn to look at numeric patterns using graphs of ordered pairs on the coordinate plane (5.OA.B.3). This skill builds throughout middle school math, as students begin to represent real-world problems using graphs and to interpret those graphs in the context of specific problems. The skills and reasoning needed to interpret those graphs will help students to interpret the features of a graph of a function as Standards 4 and 5 require. As students become adept in identifying and interpreting the key features of graphs of functions, they gain the skills needed to fit a quadratic function to a set of data to solve problems, which is content found in the conceptual category Statistics and Probability (specifically, in HSS-ID.B.6). These skills will also help students understand the content found in the Building Functions domain.

Standard 6 (HSF-IF.B.6), regarding calculating and interpreting the rate of change, builds on the foundation of previous standards in the cluster. After students calculate the average rate of change of a function, they can use their ability to interpret a function's graph in context to interpret that calculated value in context. Students are first introduced to rate problems in 6th grade, when they use ratio and rates to solve problems (6.RP.A.3). The idea that unit rate is equivalent to the slope of a graph is introduced in 8th grade (8.EE.B.5). Students' ability to calculate and interpret the average rate of change builds on the ideas presented in middle school, and it will help them model problem situations using functions (as found in the Building Functions domain).

Analyze functions using different representations

Cluster C extends students' understanding of functions to include different representations, including graphs and equivalent forms (see Figure 4.3).

Figure 4.3 | **Analyze Functions Using Different Representations**

7. Graph functions expressed symbolically and show key features of the graph, by hand in simple cases and using technology for more complicated cases. ★
   a. Graph linear and quadratic functions and show intercepts, maxima, and minima.
   b. Graph square root, cube root, and piecewise-defined functions, including step functions and absolute value functions.
   c. Graph polynomial functions, identifying zeros when suitable factorizations are available, and showing end behavior.
   d. (+) Graph rational functions, identifying zeros and asymptotes when suitable factorizations are available, and showing end behavior.
   e. Graph exponential and logarithmic functions, showing intercepts and end behavior, and trigonometric functions, showing period, midline, and amplitude.
8. Write a function defined by an expression in different but equivalent forms to reveal and explain different properties of the function.
   a. Use the process of factoring and completing the square in a quadratic function to show zeros, extreme values, and symmetry of the graph, and interpret these in terms of a context.
   b. Use the properties of exponents to interpret expressions for exponential functions. *For example, identify percent rate of change in functions such as* $y = (1.02)^t$, $y = (0.97)^t$, $y = (1.01)^{12t}$, $y = (1.2)^{\frac{t}{10}}$, *and classify them as representing exponential growth or decay.*

The graphing of linear and quadratic expressions and equations (Algebra) has many similarities to the graphing of functions, and both are developed from the same middle school skill set. The lettered component statements within Standard 7 (HSF-IF.C.7) serve to specify and sort the different types of functions by perceived difficulty level. It's clear from Appendix A (CCSSI, 2010d) that these components are sequenced to reflect the order in which students are expected to be able to graph the different types of functions. Specifically, linear, exponential, quadratic, absolute value, step, and piecewise-defined functions should be taught during students' first year or two of high school mathematics, while rational, radical, and logarithmic functions are intended for third-year courses and above. It's not completely clear which year is appropriate for logarithmic functions. In addition, there appears to be a discrepancy between the Standards for Mathematical Content and Appendix A. In the standards document, HSF-IF.C.7d focuses on rational functions and is marked as not required for all students, while HSF-IF.C.7e focuses on logarithmic and trigonometric functions. In the tables describing the courses in Appendix A, this appears to be reversed, so that content related to logarithmic functions appears in the fourth-year course only, and content related to rational functions appears in the third-year course, required of all students.

Standard 8 (HSF-IF.C.8) asks students to write functions in equivalent forms. The skills needed for this task are similar to those needed to write expressions in equivalent forms, addressed in HSA-SSE.B.3–4 (see p. 29).

There are only two standards in this cluster, and much like the standards regarding sequences described earlier, neither is designed to be taught exclusively during a single course or during a single year. Note that the components of both Standard 7 and Standard 8 contain content appropriate to specific courses designed for different grades. Therefore, the understanding and skills involved in graphing functions and writing functions in equivalent forms should be addressed across grade levels as student understanding of each type of function developes, as described in Appendix A.

Building Functions

The Building Functions domain asks students to use knowledge about functions developed in 8th grade (8.F.A.1–5) and in high school (HSF-IF). Its standards focus on developing students' ability to model a relationship between two quantities and build new functions from existing functions.

Attacking a new kind of problem invokes Mathematical Practice Standard 1 ("Make sense of problems and persevere in solving them"). To build a function from the context of a specific problem, students will need to explain the meaning of a problem and analyze givens and relationships found in that problem. In addition, connecting the building of functions to more familiar, analogous problems will help students determine the expression, process, or steps for calculation to be used. Students who use these approaches will find it easier to write functions that describe relationships, model situations with sequences, and build new functions from existing functions. The ability to understand and represent a problem both in function notation and in a problem context is evidence that students are reasoning abstractly and quantitatively (Mathematical Practice Standard 2) as well as modeling with mathematics (Mathematical Practice Standard 4). Students will also be looking for and making use of structure (Mathematical Practice Standard 7) as they build functions by combining standard function types and create new functions from existing functions. Using appropriate tools (Mathematical Practice Standard 5) to illustrate the functions they've built will help students understand how changes to functions affect their graphs.

The Building Functions domain contains five standards, organized into two clusters.

Build a function that models a relationship between two quantities

As the name of this cluster implies, its aim is to get students deeply involved in modeling (see Figure 4.4).

Figure 4.4 | **Build a Function That Models a Relationship Between Two Quantities**

HSF-BF.A

1. Write a function that describes a relationship between two quantities. ★
   a. Determine an explicit expression, a recursive process, or steps for calculation from a context.
   b. Combine standard function types using arithmetic operations. *For example, build a function that models the temperature of a cooling body by adding a constant function to a decaying exponential, and relate these functions to the model.*
   c. (+) Compose functions. *For example, if T(y) is the temperature in the atmosphere as a function of height, and h(t) is the height of a weather balloon as a function of time, then T(h(t)) is the temperature at the location of the weather balloon as a function of time.*
2. Write arithmetic and geometric sequences both recursively and with an explicit formula, use them to model situations, and translate between the two forms. ★

Both standards are marked with a ★, indicating that they're intended to be used to connect students' academic understanding of mathematical content with real-world practical problems. While working on either standard, students will connect their understanding of functions (developed in 8th grade and under the Interpreting Functions domain) with their ability to model problems. There are several interesting similarities and differences between the 8th grade cluster "Use functions to model relationships between quantities" (8.F.B) and this high school cluster (HSF-BF.A). In 8th grade, students construct linear functions, looking at rate of change both in a graph or table and in terms of the problem context. High school students will build on this, using their prior experiences with linear functions and connecting them with their more recent experiences with exponential functions, series, and sequences.

There are three content standards that specifically refer to sequences or series: HSA-SSE.B.4 ("Derive the formula for the sum of a finite geometric series"), HSF-IF.A.3 ("Recognize that sequences are functions, sometimes defined recursively, whose domain is a subset of the integers"), and this cluster's Standard 2 (HSF-BF.A.2). Please refer back to the earlier discussion of the "Understand the concept of a function and use function notation" cluster within the Interpreting Functions domain (p. 43–43) for a full look at the progression of sequences across and within grade levels.

Build new functions from existing functions

The second cluster in this domain describes how students will apply their understanding of existing functions to build new functions (see Figure 4.5).

While Cluster A of the Building Function domain focused on building functions based on relationships, Cluster B focuses on changing existing functions. Here, students learn to evaluate functions for a variety of values and are introduced to the concept of inverse functions. As the PARCC frameworks document describes, teachers can "pave the way" for this work with linear functions, allowing students to practice constructing tables of values and drawing simpler graphs by hand. PARCC also points out that the effect of replacing $f(x)$ for other values can be "interpreted geometrically," using the language of transformations (2011, p. 40). This act of transformation may help students make the leap from the simpler substitutions seen

---

Figure 4.5 | **Build New Functions from Existing Functions**

3. Identify the effect on the graph of replacing $f(x)$ by $f(x) + k$, $k\,f(x)$, $f(kx)$, and $f(x + k)$ for specific values of k (both positive and negative); find the value of k given the graphs. Experiment with cases and illustrate an explanation of the effects on the graph using technology. *Include recognizing even and odd functions from their graphs and algebraic expressions for them.*

4. Find inverse functions.

   a. Solve an equation of the form $f(x) = c$ for a simple function f that has an inverse and write an expression for the inverse. *For example, $f(x) = 2x^3$ or $f(x) = \dfrac{(x + 1)}{(x - 1)}$ for $x \neq 1$.*

   b. (+) Verify by composition that one function is the inverse of another.

   c. (+) Read values of an inverse function from a graph or a table, given that the function has an inverse.

   d. (+) Produce an invertible function from a non-invertible function by restricting the domain.

5. (+) Understand the inverse relationship between exponents and logarithms and use this relationship to solve problems involving logarithms and exponents.

---

in previous standards to the more complex substitutions and the resulting graphs asked for here, in Standard 3 (HSF-BF.B.3). Note that although students should be adept at graphing by hand, using technology such as graphing calculators or computer software will assist them as they work with more cumbersome and complex calculations, keeping the focus on making sense of problems and evaluating situations.

When students find inverse functions, they're building on their understanding of graphing and the Cartesian coordinate system. The more advanced components of Standard 4 (HSF-BF.B.4), marked with a (+), build on students' ability not only to write the expression for an inverse function but also to work with inverses using composition and restricting the domain. To assist students in understanding the composition of functions, teachers may want to review the algebraic substitution method of solving systems of equations—a skill introduced in 8th grade (8.EE.C.8) and developed further in the high school Number and Quantity and Algebra conceptual categories—and apply it to the evaluation of functions using variables and numbers. This comparison may assist students in making sense of the new types of problems.

The final standard in this cluster, Standard 5 (HSF-BF.B.5) builds on students' understanding of exponential and logarithmic functions. (Please see the discussion of the "Analyze functions using different representations" cluster in the Interpreting Functions domain—HSF-IF.C, pp. 46–48, for a description of how students' understanding of exponents and exponential functions is developed throughout the grade levels.) Here, Standard 5 asks students to make a connection between the exponential and logarithmic functions and to use that inverse relationship to build one type of function from the other in a problem-solving context.

Linear, Quadratic, and Exponential Models ★

All content within this domain focuses on modeling, as reflected both in the domain title and in the ★ symbol used to indicate content that is best suited for making mathematical models. The entire domain, then, is intended to assist students as they learn to apply what they know about linear, quadratic, and exponential functions to solve problems in practical situations, as described in Mathematical Practice Standard 4, "Model with mathematics."

The ability to model with mathematics goes hand in hand with reasoning abstractly and quantitatively (Mathematical Practice Standard 2). The various standards within this domain ask students to look at problem situations from a real-world perspective and to see the same problem situation from the quantitative (mathematical) point of view. Students will need to reason from both perspectives when they're asked to compare problem situations to determine how to model a given problem. The standards within this domain ask students to show the ability to "contextualize" the parameters of functions—that is, to make sense of them using real-world applications. This kind of contextualizing is also evidence of abstract reasoning. In addition, students are expected to look at a problem situation and "decontextualize" it to a given mathematical function—that is, determine how real-world parameters or constraints can be represented mathematically.

When students develop mathematical proofs about linear and exponential functions, whether formal or informal, they are constructing viable arguments (Mathematical Practice Standard 3) and communicating precisely to others (Mathematical Practice Standard 6). Students might find graphing technology useful for constructing and comparing functions, since it allows them to focus more on comparing than on constructing graphs—an example of using "appropriate tools strategically" (Mathematical Practice Standard 5).

This domain has five standards, grouped in two clusters.

Construct and compare linear, quadratic, and exponential models and solve problems

Students are deeply involved in modeling while working on the standards in this cluster (see Figure 4.6).

Figure 4.6 | **Construct and Compare Linear, Quadratic, and Exponential Models and Solve Problems**

HSF-LE.A

1. Distinguish between situations that can be modeled with linear functions and with exponential functions.
   a. Prove that linear functions grow by equal differences over equal intervals, and that exponential functions grow by equal factors over equal intervals.
   b. Recognize situations in which one quantity changes at a constant rate per unit interval relative to another.
   c. Recognize situations in which a quantity grows or decays by a constant percent rate per unit interval relative to another.
2. Construct linear and exponential functions, including arithmetic and geometric sequences, given a graph, a description of a relationship, or two input-output pairs (include reading these from a table).
3. Observe using graphs and tables that a quantity increasing exponentially eventually exceeds a quantity increasing linearly, quadratically, or (more generally) as a polynomial function.
4. For exponential models, express as a logarithm the solution to $ab^{ct} = d$ where a, c, and d are numbers and the base b is 2, 10, or e; evaluate the logarithm using technology.

The entire domain is marked with a ★, indicating that Standards 1–5 (HSF-LE.A.1–4, HSF-LE.B.5) are all intended to help students understand how mathematics applies to "physical, economic, public policy, social, and everyday situations" (CCSSI, 2010c, p. 72). While working on any of the four standards in Cluster A, students will learn how to use their understanding of functions, exponents, or quadratic equations to model problems. This type of application begins in middle school, as students work with expressions, equations, and functions. In high school, students build on this foundation, gaining experience with quadratic and exponential equations and functions (as described in Number and Quantity, Algebra, and the other domains in Functions). The PARCC frameworks document explains that the understanding of linear functions described in these standards will help students begin to study "linear associations in statistics and probability" found in the Interpreting Categorical and Quantitative Data domain of the Statistics and Probability category (PARCC, 2011, p. 41).

Standard 2 (HSF-LE.A.2) asks students to construct linear and exponential functions including arithmetic and geometric sequences. (For a full discussion of the progression of sequences across and within grade levels, please refer to the discussion of "Understand the concept of a function and use function notation," Cluster A within the Interpreting Functions domain, beginning on p. 43.)

Four of the five standards in this cluster are intended to be taught within the first or second year of high school mathematics. Standard 4 (HSF-LE.A.4) is designed to build on students' understanding of exponential functions in order to introduce the idea of logarithms. The course placement of the majority of content related to logarithms indicates that logarithms are generally expected to be found in third-year courses. In the current cluster on constructing and comparing models, students are asked to express solutions to specific exponential models as a logarithm. This skill is very similar to HSF-BF.B.5, marked with a (+), in which students are asked to "understand the inverse relationship between exponents and logarithms" and use that relationship to solve problems. Although the content in the Building Functions domain is marked with a (+), it appears to be content that is expected to be taught to all students.

Interpret expressions for functions in terms of the situation they model

This is another of the handful of clusters containing just a single standard (see Figure 4.7).

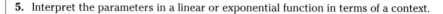

Figure 4.7 | **Interpret Expressions for Functions in Terms of the Situation They Model**

5. Interpret the parameters in a linear or exponential function in terms of a context.

HSF-LE.B

In order to successfully interpret the parameters of a linear or exponential function, students need to be very familiar with the mathematical and graphical representations of lines and exponents and functional parameters. This familiarity is built throughout the grades. (For a description of how students' understanding of exponents and exponential functions is developed throughout the grade levels, please see the discussion of "Analyze functions using different representations," Cluster C within the Interpreting Functions domain, beginning on page 46.) Standard 5 (HSF-LE.B.5) asks students to *interpret* linear and exponential functions in context, a skill that is very much related to the content of HSA-SSE.A.1 in the Algebra category. Interpreting expressions for functions in terms of a situation is also similar to the content found in HSF-IF.B, in which students are asked to interpret key features of graphs and tables in terms of the quantities and relate the domain of a function to its graph. Teachers may want to address Standard 5 in conjunction with HSA.SSE.A.1 and with HSF-BF.B.3, which asks students to identify the effect on graphs of replacing different parameters of a function. Combined, these three standards help students interpret parameters in a context.

Trigonometric Functions

This fourth domain within the Functions concept category extends students' abilities to work with trigonometric identities by introducing the concept of the unit circle and radian measure, asking students to model with trigonometric functions and to prove and apply trigonometric identities. Doing so builds on students' understanding of right angle trigonometry, developed within the conceptual area of Geometry, as well as skills they've acquired while working with functions, described in previous Functions domains.

As students use the understanding and skills they developed in previous courses to explain how unit circles enable the extension of trigonometric functions to all real numbers or to solve trigonometric equations in modeling contexts, they may participate in activities such as considering analogous problems or "analyzing givens, constraints, relationships, or goals," which are described in the Common Core as aspects of Mathematical Practice Standard 1. When students begin to engage in modeling problems involving periodic phenomena, they will benefit from their ability to shift perspectives on mathematical problems, developed throughout K–12 mathematics. When students choose which trigonometric functions would best be used to model the phenomena involved, they're thinking about the problem context as well as thinking about the different types of trigonometric functions. This ability to shift viewpoints, or reason abstractly and quantitatively, is a skill identified in Mathematical Practice Standard 2.

There's a further connection to the practice standards in Cluster C of this domain, under which students "prove and apply trigonometric identities." When students develop proofs—whether formal or informal—about the trigonometric identities while constructing a logical chain of reasoning using clear and precise mathematical language and detail, they are engaging in the development of viable arguments (Mathematical Practice Standard 3) and attending to precision (Mathematical Practice Standard 6). As they develop the proof for the Pythagorean identity, students will find it helpful to be able to see the parts of an equation as separate entities that are also related to the whole. This ability to see the "sub-expressions" in the identities will allow students to work more fluently as they develop their proofs, an important component of Mathematical Practice Standard 7. In addition, the ★ appended to Standard 5 (HSF-TF.B.5) and Standard 7 (HSF-TF.B.7) of Trigonometric Functions identifies them as modeling standards, and, thus, directly related to Mathematical Practice Standard 4.

The domain has nine standards, which are organized into three clusters.

Extend the domain of trigonometric functions using the unit circle

Cluster A of Trigonometric Functions (see Figure 4.8) connects the ideas about right angles found in geometry standards to unit circles and radian measures.

Figure 4.8 | Extend the Domain of Trigonometric Functions Using the Unit Circle

1. Understand radian measure of an angle as the length of the arc on the unit circle subtended by the angle.
2. Explain how the unit circle in the coordinate plane enables the extension of trigonometric functions to all real numbers, interpreted as radian measures of angles traversed counterclockwise around the unit circle.
3. (+) Use special triangles to determine geometrically the values of sine, cosine, tangent for $\pi/3, \pi/4$ and $\pi/6$ and use the unit circle to express the values of sine, cosine, and tangent for $\pi - x$, $\pi + x$, and $2\pi - x$ in terms of their values for x, where x is any real number.
4. (+) Use the unit circle to explain symmetry (odd and even) and periodicity of trigonometric functions.

Standard 1 (HSF-TF.A.1) and Standard 2 (HSF-TF.A.2) address content that is common in college readiness standards but was not typically required learning for all students prior to the adoption of the Common Core standards.

Standard 3 (HSF-TF.A.3) and Standard 4 (HSF-TF.A.4) are marked with a (+), indicating that they are intended only for students continuing on to advanced mathematics courses such as Calculus. These students will benefit from the ability to work with special triangles and to use the unit circle to explain symmetry and the periodicity of trigonometric functions. As students begin to work with these more advanced concepts, they may find it helpful to connect the newer ways of thinking about trigonometric functions to the concepts found in Geometry regarding trigonometric functions. They may also find it useful to connect the understanding they've developed for recognizing even and odd functions (developed in HSF-BF.B.3) as they learn about even and odd trigonometric functions.

> For an example of an Algebra II or Mathematics III lesson that addresses HSF-TF.A.1 and HSF-TF.A.2, see **Sample Lesson 3**.

Model periodic phenomena with trigonometric functions

Cluster B within this domain asks students to apply their understanding of trigonometric functions to model periodic phenomena (see Figure 4.9).

HSF-TF.B

Figure 4.9 | **Model Periodic Phenomena with Trigonometric Functions**

5. Choose trigonometric functions to model periodic phenomena with specified amplitude, frequency, and midline. ★
6. (+) Understand that restricting a trigonometric function to a domain on which it is always increasing or always decreasing allows its inverse to be constructed.
7. (+) Use inverse functions to solve trigonometric equations that arise in modeling contexts; evaluate the solutions using technology, and interpret them in terms of the context. ★

As the name of this cluster implies, students are deeply involved in modeling while working on this set of standards. As noted on page 56 and shown in the figure, two of the three standards are marked with a ★, indicating that they are intended to connect students' understanding of mathematical content with "physical, economic, public policy, social, and everyday situations" (CCSSI, 2010c, p. 72). Certain phrases in the standards such as "periodic phenomena" and "modeling contexts" underscore the Common Core writers' intent to make clear connections to modeling standards.

We can see in Standard 5 (HSF-TF.B.5) that students will be connecting their understanding of trigonometric functions with their ability to model problems using functions. This understanding and ability have been built from Geometry content focused on trigonometry, content in Cluster A of this domain regarding radian measures, and the ability to interpret and build functions, as described in the first two domains of the Functions conceptual category. In Appendix A, the Common Core writers suggest that Standard 5 be taught in the third year of high school mathematics (Algebra II or Mathematics III). Standard 6 (HSF-TF.B.6) and Standard 7 (HSF-TF.B.7), marked with a (+), are intended for an optional fourth-year course and will deepen students' understanding about inverse trigonometric functions in contextual situations.

Prove and apply trigonometric identities

Cluster C in the Trigonometric Functions domain addresses proofs of trigonometric identities (see Figure 4.10).

Figure 4.10 | Prove and Apply Trigonometric Identities

HSF-TF.C

8. Prove the Pythagorean identity $\sin^2(\theta) + \cos^2(\theta) = 1$ and use it to find $\sin(\theta)$, $\cos(\theta)$, or $\tan(\theta)$ given $\sin(\theta)$, $\cos(\theta)$, or $\tan(\theta)$ and the quadrant of the angle.

9. (+) Prove the addition and subtraction formulas for sine, cosine, and tangent and use them to solve problems.

In grade 8, students learn to prove the Pythagorean Theorem and apply it to real-world and mathematical problems (8.G.C.6–8). Appendix A states that students in high school courses Algebra I or Integrated Mathematics I are expected to be able to interpret complicated expressions and use the structure of an expression as a way to rewrite it. Students are introduced to basic trigonometric ratios in their second year of high school math, Geometry or Integrated Mathematics II. Standard 8 (HSF-TF.C.8) in this cluster, which is placed in a later course—Algebra II or Mathematics III, expands upon the knowledge and skills developed in those previous grades. Students will find it helpful to use their understanding of the Pythagorean Theorem, their skills in manipulating equations, and the definitions of the trigonometric ratios as they prove the Pythagorean identity.

While the content in Standard 8 is required of all students, Standard 9 (HSF-TF.C.9) is marked with a (+), which indicates that it is not required and is not designated for assessment by the assessment consortia. In order to perform a proof of the addition and subtraction formulas for the trigonometric functions, students will need a deep understanding of the concepts found in the Geometry domain Similarity, Right Triangles, and Trigonometry, which we will look at in the next chapter. This understanding will help them as they continue on to Calculus or other advanced mathematics courses.

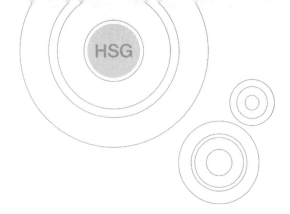

CHAPTER 5

Geometry

Each introduction to the different conceptual areas in the Common Core document contains helpful information, but the introduction to Geometry is particularly informative, so be sure to read it. It contains useful insights into the development of the Geometry section and explains the logical progression of concepts as laid out in the domain. In this chapter, we will lean heavily on the Geometry introduction as we review each domain, identifying the connections between mathematical content and mathematical practices and considering how the content differs and builds across grades and conceptual areas.

The following domains appear within the conceptual category of Geometry (HSG):

- Congruence (HSG-CO)
- Similarity, Right Triangles, and Trigonometry (HSG-SRT)
- Circles (HSG-C)
- Expressing Geometric Properties with Equations (HSG-GPE)
- Geometric Measurement and Dimension (HSG-GMD)
- Modeling with Geometry (HSG-MG)

Taken together, these domains are designed to help students develop an understanding of geometric definitions, attributes, and reasoning. Unlike the first few conceptual categories in the Common Core (Number and Quantity, Algebra, and Functions), the content found in Geometry can be used as the basis for a course without incorporating a large amount of additional content from another conceptual category. In other words, while every other conceptual category contains standards intended to be mixed with those from other conceptual categories in first- or second-year high school math courses, Geometry stands alone. Although the content may relate to knowledge and skills found in Algebra (e.g., completing the square), Functions (e.g., radians), or Number and Quantity (e.g., unit analysis), the conceptual category of Geometry is much more self-contained than the other categories. As described in the introduction to Geometry, as well as in Appendix A of the standards document (CCSSI, 2010d), students will extend previous skills and understanding developed in middle school to deepen their understanding of the Euclidean geometry system.

Each of the domains in Geometry builds on the ones preceding it. As described in the Geometry introduction, the first three domains focus on the fundamental tools used to formalize students' understanding about the concepts of congruence, similarity, and symmetry, from the perspective of geometric transformations. The final three domains use the coordinate system to connect algebraic and geometric concepts, providing students with powerful problem-solving tools.

We'll now look at each domain in greater detail.

Congruence

As described in the introduction to Geometry, the Congruence domain formalizes and extends the geometric knowledge and skills that students have developed throughout the middle school grades. The skills learned while studying the concepts in this domain—transformations, congruence, geometric theorems, and geometric constructions—will be the basis for students' understanding of the concepts found in the remaining domains.

Not only do the standards within this domain connect across grade levels and other Geometry domains, but they also offer multiple opportunities for students to engage in the mathematical practice standards. For example, as students use their knowledge about the different properties of geometric objects to reason about various definitions, theorems, and applications, they're applying an important aspect of Mathematical Practice Standard 2, "Reason abstractly and quantitatively." The abilities to explain how given geometrical criteria follow logically from a definition, to develop definitions or geometric proofs, and to make a prediction about a transformation are all directly related to constructing viable arguments (Mathematical Practice Standard 3) and communicating precisely to others (Mathematical Practice Standard 6). Students should have the opportunity to "use appropriate tools strategically" (Mathematical Practice Standard 5) in several places throughout the domain as they draw or represent transformations and develop formal geometric constructions using a wide variety of tools. As students transform or construct geometric objects, Mathematical Practice Standard 7 ("Look for and make use of structure") will help them see geometric shapes as combinations of several objects.

The Congruence domain has 13 standards, organized into four clusters.

Experiment with transformations in the plane

The introduction to the Geometry conceptual category explains that "the concepts of congruence, similarity, and symmetry can be understood from the perspective of geometric transformation" (CCSSI, 2010c, p. 74). From that perspective, the standards within this first cluster (see Figure 5.1) represent the basis for all other content within Geometry. While students have been working with geometric shapes and transformations prior to high school, here they are asked to solidify their grasp of key concepts and develop the geometric understandings they will need to develop formal proofs.

Note the difference between 8th grade expectations and the expectations found at the high school level. Although the standards within the high school cluster contain ideas that appear in the 8th grade standards, such as developing a physical understanding of congruence and similarity

Figure 5.1 | **Experiment with Transformations in the Plane**

1. Know precise definitions of angle, circle, perpendicular line, parallel line, and line segment, based on the undefined notions of point, line, distance along a line, and distance around a circular arc.

2. Represent transformations in the plane using, e.g., transparencies and geometry software; describe transformations as functions that take points in the plane as inputs and give other points as outputs. Compare transformations that preserve distance and angle to those that do not (e.g., translation versus horizontal stretch).

3. Given a rectangle, parallelogram, trapezoid, or regular polygon, describe the rotations and reflections that carry it onto itself.

4. Develop definitions of rotations, reflections, and translations in terms of angles, circles, perpendicular lines, parallel lines, and line segments.

5. Given a geometric figure and a rotation, reflection, or translation, draw the transformed figure using, e.g., graph paper, tracing paper, or geometry software. Specify a sequence of transformations that will carry a given figure onto another.

using models and demonstrating sequences of transformations, observing properties, and determining what sequence of transformations can illustrate the congruence of two figures, definitions are formalized, and the transformation of figures is connected to the idea of functions.

Understand congruence in terms of rigid motions

Proceeding directly from the fundamental definitions and skills developed in earlier grades and addressed in the domain's first cluster, the second cluster focuses on the idea that congruence can be understood in terms of rigid motions (see Figure 5.2).

As with the previous cluster, the skills and understanding addressed here, in Cluster B, have their immediate roots in the ability to represent transformations in the plane and to explain how reflections and rotations can carry an object onto another object. The understanding of congruence in terms of rigid motion was developed first in the 8th grade standard 8.G.A.2. Once students have learned what the transformed object

HSG-CO.B

Figure 5.2 | **Understand Congruence in Terms of Rigid Motions**

6. Use geometric descriptions of rigid motions to transform figures and to predict the effect of a given rigid motion on a given figure; given two figures, use the definition of congruence in terms of rigid motions to decide if they are congruent.

7. Use the definition of congruence in terms of rigid motions to show that two triangles are congruent if and only if corresponding pairs of sides and corresponding pairs of angles are congruent.

8. Explain how the criteria for triangle congruence (ASA, SAS, and SSS) follow from the definition of congruence in terms of rigid motions.

looks like when certain rigid motions have been performed, they'll be able to use the descriptions of rigid motions to predict the effects of a given transformation, the skill presented in Standard 6 (HSG-CO.B.6). The standards in this cluster ask students to use their understanding of the definition of congruence to develop more formal definitions for triangle congruence. This application also draws on students' work in 7th grade, when they're asked to construct triangles from three measures of angles or sides and make note of the resulting shapes (7.G.A.2).

Prove geometric theorems

Once students have become familiar with the criteria for congruence and the formal definitions of geometric terms, they can begin to develop proofs of specific geometric theorems, as described in Cluster C of this domain (see Figure 5.3).

Having students prove geometric theorems about lines, angles, triangles, and parallelograms will build on the understanding of geometric objects and congruence they developed in the domain's first two clusters. In 8th grade, students were asked to use informal arguments to establish facts about transversal lines and the angle-angle criterion for similarity of triangles (8.G.A.5) and were introduced to proofs when they were tasked with explaining a proof of the Pythagorean Theorem (8.G.B.6). The standards in this cluster now ask the student to develop proofs. As students

---

Figure 5.3 | **Prove Geometric Theorems**

9. Prove theorems about lines and angles. *Theorems include: vertical angles are congruent; when a transversal crosses parallel lines, alternate interior angles are congruent and corresponding angles are congruent; points on a perpendicular bisector of a line segment are exactly those equidistant from the segment's endpoints.*

10. Prove theorems about triangles. *Theorems include: measures of interior angles of a triangle sum to 180°; base angles of isosceles triangles are congruent; the segment joining midpoints of two sides of a triangle is parallel to the third side and half the length; the medians of a triangle meet at a point.*

11. Prove theorems about parallelograms. *Theorems include: opposite sides are congruent, opposite angles are congruent, the diagonals of a parallelogram bisect each other, and conversely, rectangles are parallelograms with congruent diagonals.*

---

become more familiar with how to construct proofs, they will develop their ability to reason and analyze situations, tactics that will serve them well in later courses, both in and outside mathematics.

Make geometric constructions

In the domain's final cluster (see Figure 5.4), students continue to develop more formal constructions of geometric options.

Figure 5.4 | **Make Geometric Constructions**

12. Make formal geometric constructions with a variety of tools and methods (compass and straightedge, string, reflective devices, paper folding, dynamic geometric software, etc.). *Copying a segment; copying an angle; bisecting a segment; bisecting an angle; constructing perpendicular lines, including the perpendicular bisector of a line segment; and constructing a line parallel to a given line through a point not on the line.*

13. Construct an equilateral triangle, a square, and a regular hexagon inscribed in a circle.

For years, students have been developing an informal understanding of the skills presented in these two standards. In 7th grade, for example, they were asked to draw geometric shapes with given conditions freehand, with a ruler, and with technology (7.G.A.2). Now, students must apply the skills they acquired in those earlier grades and combine them with the more formal understanding developed in the first three clusters of the Congruence domain. Comfort with the definitions and applications found within this domain will prepare students to define "similarity," which is explored in the next domain.

Similarity, Right Triangles, and Trigonometry

This domain formalizes students' understanding about similarity developed in middle school math courses and adds to the more formal definitions developed in the first Geometry domain. In 7th grade, students reproduce a scale drawing at a different scale, informally introducing them to the idea of dilation (7.G.A.1); in 8th grade, students are introduced to the informal understanding of similarity as a sequence of rigid motions followed by dilations (8.G.A). The formal definitions and construction skills introduced in the first high school Geometry domain combine with the informal understandings from middle school to allow students to extend their understanding of similarity, prove theorems involving similarity, and understand trigonometric ratios in terms of similarity. This, in combination with triangular congruence criteria and algebraic concepts, will allow students to apply trigonometry to general triangles.

As students begin to delve deeply into similarity, right triangles, and trigonometry by developing proofs, deriving formulas, and solving problems, they're engaging in activities related to Mathematical Practice Standard 1, making sense of problems by analyzing givens, constraints, relationships, and goals related to the proofs or problems. Those same proofs, derivations, and problems give students an opportunity to know and flexibly use the different properties of objects, thus engaging them in Mathematical Practice Standard 2, "Reason abstractly and quantitatively." The abilities to explain how given geometrical criteria follow logically from a definition, to develop definitions or geometric proofs, and to derive a formula are all directly related to the ability of students to construct viable arguments (Mathematical Practice Standard 3) and communicate precisely to others (Mathematical Practice Standard 6). Students should have the opportunity to strategically use appropriate tools (Mathematical Practice Standard 5) in several places throughout the domain as they draw or represent transformations and dilations. In addition, they will develop the ability to see geometric shapes as combinations of several objects, a skill associated with Mathematical Practice Standard 7, "Look for and make use of structure."

This domain has 11 standards, grouped into four clusters.

Understand similarity in terms of similarity transformations

The first cluster (see Figure 5.5) extends informal understandings first addressed in middle school Geometry.

Figure 5.5 │ **Understand Similarity in Terms of Similarity Transformations**

1. Verify experimentally the properties of dilations given by a center and a scale factor:
   a. A dilation takes a line not passing through the center of the dilation to a parallel line, and leaves a line passing through the center unchanged.
   b. The dilation of a line segment is longer or shorter in the ratio given by the scale factor.
2. Given two figures, use the definition of similarity in terms of similarity transformations to decide if they are similar; explain using similarity transformations the meaning of similarity for triangles as the equality of all corresponding pairs of angles and the proportionality of all corresponding pairs of sides.
3. Use the properties of similarity transformations to establish the AA criterion for two triangles to be similar.

Standard 1 (HSG-SRT.A.1) and Standard 2 (HSG-SRT.A.2) extend the understanding of scale factors and similarity students developed in middle school by asking them to verify fundamental properties of dilations and to use the definition of similarity to decide on the similarity of shapes. Standard 3 (HSG-SRT.A.3) appears very similar to an 8th grade standard, 8.G.A.5, which asks students to "use informal arguments to establish *facts about* . . . the angle-angle (AA) criterion for similarity of triangles" (emphasis added). Standard 3 goes beyond that expectation, asking students to establish the AA criterion itself. To master these standards, students will need to apply understanding and formal definitions acquired through work on the standards in the Congruence domain.

Prove theorems involving similarity

Once students are familiar with the definition of similarity and the properties of dilations, they are ready to engage in the work outlined in this cluster: the development of proofs about theorems involving similarity (see Figure 5.6).

HSG-SRT.B

Figure 5.6 | **Prove Theorems Involving Similarity**

4. Prove theorems about triangles. *Theorems include: a line parallel to one side of a triangle divides the other two proportionally, and conversely; the Pythagorean Theorem proved using triangle similarity.*
5. Use congruence and similarity criteria for triangles to solve problems and to prove relationships in geometric figures.

Proving geometric theorems about triangles will build on students' understanding of the definitions of geometric objects and similarity developed in the first cluster of this domain. In addition, the shift from explaining a proof of the Pythagorean Theorem in 8th grade (8.G.B.6) to developing such a proof as required by Standard 4 (HSG-SRT.B.4) is consistent with the increased emphasis on the development of proofs found throughout the high school courses (see also the Functions and Algebra categories). As students become more adept at constructing proofs, they will improve their ability to reason and analyze problem situations.

Define trigonometric ratios and solve problems involving right triangles

The content found in Cluster C of the Similarity, Right Triangles, and Trigonometry domain (see Figure 5.7) introduces students to trigonometric ratios. It also leverages students' understanding of similarity and of the properties of triangles—as described in the domain's previous clusters—to help them develop a deeper understanding of why trigonometric ratios work for all right triangles—that is, why the ratio of two sides is always a constant for a given acute angle.

Figure 5.7　ǀ　**Define Trigonometric Ratios and Solve Problems Involving Right Triangles**

6.　Understand that by similarity, side ratios in right triangles are properties of the angles in the triangle, leading to definitions of trigonometric ratios for acute angles.

7.　Explain and use the relationship between the sine and cosine of complementary angles.

8.　Use trigonometric ratios and the Pythagorean Theorem to solve right triangles in applied problems. ★

Standard 7 (HSG-SRT.C.7) asks students to use their understanding about complementary angles and relate it to their new knowledge of trigonometric ratios. Understanding of complementary angles is first addressed in 7th grade (7.G.B.5) when students are asked to use facts about complementary angles in multistep problems to solve for an unknown angle. This understanding is further developed in the first Geometry domain, as students prove theorems about lines and angles.

The final standard in this cluster, Standard 8 (HSG-SRT.C.8), is marked with a ★, indicating that it is intended to be used to connect students' understanding of mathematical content with "physical, economic, public policy, social, and everyday situations" (CCSSI, 2010c, p. 72), providing context for the standards writers' reference to "applied problems." The content in this standard is an extension of that found in 8th grade, when students apply the Pythagorean Theorem to real-world and mathematical problems (8.G.B). In their future schooling and work, students should find their understanding of the Pythagorean Theorem and trigonometric ratios to have many practical applications, such as determining angles of elevation or depression. Within the mathematical standards, this fundamental understanding of trigonometric ratios will assist them as they move on to more advanced high school courses in which they are asked to work with trigonometric functions.

Apply trigonometry to general triangles

All content within this fourth and final cluster in the Similarity, Right Triangles, and Trigonometry domain (see Figure 5.8) is marked with a (+), indicating that it is considered advanced content that not all students are required to learn and that is not designated for assessment by the assessment consortia.

HSG-SRT.D

Figure 5.8 | **Apply Trigonometry to General Triangles**

9. (+) Derive the formula $A = 1/2\ ab \sin(C)$ for the area of a triangle by drawing an auxiliary line from a vertex perpendicular to the opposite side.
10. (+) Prove the Laws of Sines and Cosines and use them to solve problems.
11. (+) Understand and apply the Law of Sines and the Law of Cosines to find unknown measurements in right and non-right triangles (e.g., surveying problems, resultant forces).

Standard 9 (HSG-SRT.D.9), Standard 10 (HSG-SRT.D.10), and Standard 11 (HSG-SRT.D.11) ask students to combine what they know about trigonometric ratios with their understanding of the properties of geometric objects and more advanced algebraic concepts. These standards allow students to extend their skills in solving problems involving triangles by generalizing the Pythagorean Theorem to non-right triangles using the Law of Cosines.

Appendix A of the standards document (CCSSI, 2010d) makes clear that Cluster C in this domain (Standards HSG-SRT.C.6–8), introducing basic trigonometric ratios, should be taught in students' second year of high school math (Geometry or Mathematics II) and that reasoning with complicated equations (Algebra) and advanced trigonometric concepts (Functions) should be taught in third-year mathematics courses (Algebra II or Mathematics III). Note that all standards here in Cluster D are marked with a (+), indicating that they are meant for a fourth-year course and not intended for all students. The introduction to Geometry describes some uses for the Laws of Sines and Cosines, explaining that

> Together, the Laws of Sines and Cosines embody the triangle congruence criteria for the cases where three pieces of information suffice to completely solve a triangle. Furthermore, these laws yield two possible solutions in the ambiguous case, illustrating that Side-Side-Angle is not a congruence criterion. (CCSSI, 2010c, p. 74)

The next domain in the conceptual category of Geometry moves students' focus from triangles to circles.

Circles

The first two Geometry domains—Congruence and Similarity, Right Triangles, and Trigonometry—focus primarily on building the fundamental tools for formalizing students' understanding about the concepts of congruence, similarity, and symmetry using the perspective of geometric transformations. They also concentrate on lines, angles, triangles, and parallelograms. Now the Circles domain extends the concepts of similarity and formal construction to circles.

The standards in this domain present lesson planners with a wealth of opportunities to incorporate the Standards for Mathematical Practice. As students begin to understand and apply theorems about circles, they will also begin to apply the tools that they used when solving analogous problems from previous domains regarding the proofs and construction of lines, angles, triangles, and quadrilaterals. As students use their understanding about the different properties of circles, lines, and angles to reason about the relationships among the inscribed parts, they're participating in an important aspect of Mathematical Practice Standard 2, "Reason abstractly and quantitatively." In addition, the ability to develop geometric proofs or derive formulas is directly related to students' ability to construct viable arguments (Mathematical Practice Standard 3) and communicate precisely to others (Mathematical Practice Standard 6).

The Circles domain contains five standards, organized into two clusters.

Understand and apply theorems about circles

This first cluster in the Circles domain focuses on geometrical theorems related to circles (see Figure 5.9).

HSG-C.A

Figure 5.9 | **Understand and Apply Theorems About Circles**

1. Prove that all circles are similar.
2. Identify and describe relationships among inscribed angles, radii, and chords. *Include the relationship between central, inscribed, and circumscribed angles; inscribed angles on a diameter are right angles; the radius of a circle is perpendicular to the tangent where the radius intersects the circle.*
3. Construct the inscribed and circumscribed circles of a triangle, and prove properties of angles for a quadrilateral inscribed in a circle.
4. (+) Construct a tangent line from a point outside a given circle to the circle.

As students develop the proof referenced in Standard 1 (HSG-C.A.1) they'll extend the concepts found in the first two Geometry domains around transformations, dilations, and similarity to circles. When working on Standards 2 and 3 (HSG-C.A.2–3), students draw on previous knowledge of circles developed in middle school about a circle's parts and the relationship between the circumference and the area of a circle (7.G.B.4). These formal definitions and construction skills, introduced in high school in the Congruence domain, build on students' informal understandings from middle school.

Standard 4 (HSG-C.A.4) is marked with a (+); not all students are required to learn it, and it is not designated for assessment by the assessment consortia. This standard builds on the other standards in this cluster and may be useful to students as they work with advanced mathematical constructions and proofs in a fourth-year course.

Find arc lengths and areas of sectors of circles

The skills related to proofs and construction and a solid grasp of the relationships among the parts of a circle will also support mastery of the single standard in this cluster (see Figure 5.10).

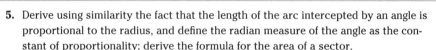

Figure 5.10 | **Find Arc Lengths and Areas of Sectors of Circles**

5. Derive using similarity the fact that the length of the arc intercepted by an angle is proportional to the radius, and define the radian measure of the angle as the constant of proportionality; derive the formula for the area of a sector.

As students develop the derivations described here in Standard 5 (HSG-C.B.5), they'll extend the concepts found in the first two domains around similarity to the parts of circles. When working on this standard, students draw on previous knowledge developed in middle school about a circle's parts, the relationship between the circumference and the area of a circle (7.G.B.4), and the concept of proportionality (6.RP.A, 7.RP.A, 8.EE.B). These skills will help students work with advanced mathematical constructions and proofs.

Expressing Geometric Properties with Equations

This domain is the first of the Geometry domains to address analytic geometry. As described in the standards document's Geometry category introduction, analytic geometry provides a connection between algebra and geometry, providing students with powerful logical tools to use when solving real-world and mathematical problems. The PARCC frameworks document names fluency with the use of coordinates one of the "most valuable tools in mathematics and related fields" (2011, p. 55).

Given the emphasis placed on this domain, teachers may want to spend extra time with these concepts to ensure that students have a strong grounding in them. Teachers can assist students in developing fluency when working with coordinates by helping them to understand and use the correspondence between numerical coordinates and geometric points, which allows methods from Algebra to be applied to geometrical objects.

As students translate between the descriptions of geometric objects and the equations for those objects, they're engaging in Mathematical Practice Standard 2, "Reason abstractly and quantitatively." Students who can use stated assumptions, definitions, and previously established mathematical tools to demonstrate the derivation of an equation and to develop geometric proofs are illustrating skills related to Mathematical Practice Standards 3 and 6. There's a further connection to the mathematical practices when students derive the equations for conic sections, because both the ability to notice a pattern or structure and the ability to step back for an overview and shift perspective are useful skills for developing derivations and are important aspects of Mathematical Practice Standard 7, "Look for and make use of structure."

This domain contains seven standards in two clusters.

Translate between the geometric description and the equation for a conic section

Cluster A of the domain focuses on the relationship between the geometric description of a circle, parabola, ellipse, or hyperbola and the equation of those conic sections (see Figure 5.11).

The first standard here, Standard 1 (HSG-GPE.A.1) asks students to bring together three concepts previously found in different places in the standards—circles, the Pythagorean Theorem, and completing the square—to derive the equation of a circle. Circles are first introduced in 7th grade (7.G.B.4), and their properties are further described in the Circles domain in Geometry. Students begin using the Pythagorean Theorem in 8th grade

---

Figure 5.11 | **Translate Between the Geometric Description and the Equation for a Conic Section**

---

1. Derive the equation of a circle of given center and radius using the Pythagorean Theorem; complete the square to find the center and radius of a circle given by an equation.
2. Derive the equation of a parabola given a focus and directrix.
3. (+) Derive the equations of ellipses and hyperbolas given the foci, using the fact that the sum or difference of distances from the foci is constant.

(8.G.B). Completing the square (HSA-SSE.A.2, HSA-SSE.B.3) is introduced in the first or second year of high school mathematics (Algebra I or Mathematics II). These background skills and knowledge will help students work within the coordinate system and derive the equation of a circle.

Standard 2 (HSG-GPE.A.2) asks students to blend algebraic and geometric concepts developed under the middle and high school Geometry standards to derive the equation for a parabola. Appendix A clarifies that, for this standard, the directrix should be parallel to the coordinate axis.

Standard 3 (HSG-GPE.A.3) is marked with a (+), indicating that it is considered advanced content and that not all students are required to learn it. This standard further develops students' abilities to work with conic sections, adding the equations of ellipses and hyperbolas to students' repertoire, which will be useful as they progress through advanced mathematics or science courses.

Use coordinates to prove simple geometric theorems algebraically

The next cluster (see Figure 5.12) describes how students will interpret relationships using algebraic equations.

The first two standards here in Cluster B, Standard 4 (HSG-GPE.B.4) and Standard 5 (HSG-GPE.B.5), ask students to use the rectangular coordinate system to prove geometric theorems algebraically, including theorems involving the properties of quadrilaterals and the slopes of lines. The definitions and theorems developed in the earlier Geometry domains

Figure 5.12 | **Use Coordinates to Prove Simple Geometric Theorems Algebraically**

4. Use coordinates to prove simple geometric theorems algebraically. *For example, prove or disprove that a figure defined by four given points in the coordinate plane is a rectangle; prove or disprove that the point (1, $\sqrt{3}$) lies on the circle centered at the origin and containing the point (0, 2).*

5. Prove the slope criteria for parallel and perpendicular lines and use them to solve geometric problems (e.g., find the equation of a line parallel or perpendicular to a given line that passes through a given point).

6. Find the point on a directed line segment between two given points that partitions the segment in a given ratio.

7. Use coordinates to compute perimeters of polygons and areas of triangles and rectangles, e.g., using the distance formula. ★

will help students develop these proofs. Appendix A offers a number of insights about the standards within this cluster, noting that work on Standard 4 should include simple proofs involving circles; work on Standard 5 should be related to work on HSA-REI.C.5 in high school Algebra I (or Mathematics I) involving systems of equations having no solutions or infinitely many solutions; and work on triangles in Standard 7 (HSG-GPE.B.7) should be limited to right triangles, which provides practice with the distance formula and its connection with the Pythagorean Theorem. Although the text of Standard 7 doesn't specify that students are to compute perimeter and area in context, the ★ provides some guidance about the writers' intent—to connect students' understanding of mathematical content with "physical, economic, public policy, social, and everyday situations" (CCSSI, 2010c, p. 72). The triangles and rectangles for which students are asked to find perimeter and area, then, should be placed into a Modeling context. The content in this standard is an extension of the content found in 8th grade, when students are asked to apply the Pythagorean Theorem to find distances (8.G.B.8). In their future schooling and work, students will find that their understanding of the Pythagorean Theorem, perimeter, and area has many practical applications.

In the next domain, students extend their work from two-dimensional objects to three-dimensional objects.

Geometric Measurement and Dimension

This is the second domain to focus on analytical geometry, building on the concepts found in the previous domain to include three-dimensional shapes. Students' foundational work with three-dimensional objects occurs mainly in middle school mathematics. In 6th and 7th grades, students learn to solve real-world problems involving right rectangular prisms using a variety of methods (6.G.A.2, 7.G.B.6), and in 8th grade, this problem solving is extended to cones, cylinders, and spheres (8.G.C.9). In addition to working with volume formulas, students in 7th grade are asked to develop insights into the relationship between two- and three-dimensional shapes. This previous learning, coupled with the algebraic work found in the high school Algebra category, will help students begin to work with the newer aspects of the topics found here in the Geometric Measurement and Dimension domain.

Under this domain, as students use their knowledge about the different properties of geometric objects to reason about various definitions, theorems, and applications, they're engaging in an important aspect of Mathematical Practice Standard 2, "Reason abstractly and quantitatively." The ability to explain how given geometrical criteria follow logically from a definition, to develop definitions or geometric proofs, or to make a prediction about a transformation is directly related to students' ability to construct viable arguments (Mathematical Practice Standard 3) and communicate precisely to others (Mathematical Practice Standard 6).

The Geometric Measurement and Dimension domain has four standards, organized into two clusters.

Explain volume formulas and use them to solve problems

In many sets of mathematical standards, there's no recognition of the reasoning students must engage in when working with volume formulas. By contrast, the standards within Cluster A of this domain (see Figure 5.13) take care to emphasize that students are not simply using volume formulas but are expected to justify the formulas using a mathematical argument.

This cluster's emphasis on expressing the reasoning process is not unusual within the Common Core mathematics standards. From the 1st grade on, the standards explicitly expect students to explain the

Figure 5.13 | **Explain Volume Formulas and Use Them to Solve Problems**

1. Give an informal argument for the formulas for the circumference of a circle, area of a circle, volume of a cylinder, pyramid, and cone. *Use dissection arguments, Cavalieri's principle, and informal limit arguments.*
2. (+) Give an informal argument using Cavalieri's principle for the formulas for the volume of a sphere and other solid figures.
3. Use volume formulas for cylinders, pyramids, cones, and spheres to solve problems. ★

mathematical concepts they're learning, along with their thought processes. The use of mathematical arguments is part of the Standards for Mathematical Practice, and, as such, it can be linked to various content standards throughout all grade levels. However, using a mathematical argument is first introduced as a content standard in 8th grade, within the Geometry domain (8.G.A.5). After that introduction, the use of arguments is found in several places in the high school content standards: as a possible method of proving theorems (HSA-APR.C.5); as a justification for a solution method (HSA-REI.A.1); and, of course, as a method to explain formulas, as in the first two standards in this cluster. Although, as noted, the use of formal argumentation should be integrated throughout a students' mathematics education, along with the rest of the mathematical practice standards, it is most emphasized in high school. In addition, within the high school conceptual standards, argumentation is more heavily emphasized in just a few domains. Appendix A provides some guidance for Standard 1 (HSG-GMD.A.1) giving a more detailed explanation of informal arguments for area and volume formulas:

> Informal arguments for area and volume formulas can make use of the way in which area and volume scale under similarity transformations; when one figure in the plane results from the other by applying a similarity transformation with scale factor k, its area is k^2 times the area of the first. Similarly, volumes of solid figures scale by k^3 under a similarity transformation with scale factor k. (CCSSI, 2010d, p. 32)

This suggested approach to the argument draws upon student understanding of the similarity and scaling content found in the second Geometry domain, Similarity, Right Triangles, and Trigonometry.

Standard 2 (HSG-GMD.A.2) is marked with a (+), indicating that it is considered mathematical content that students should know in order to take advanced courses. This standard extends the first standard to include spheres and other solid figures. Students' work with Cavalieri's principle can be considered an early step toward integral calculus.

Standard 3 (HSG-GMD.A.3) is a direct extension of skills students built in middle school. In 6th and 7th grades, students learn to solve real-world problems involving right rectangular prisms using a variety of methods (6.G.A.2, 7.G.B.6). In 8th grade, this knowledge is extended to cones, cylinders, and spheres (8.G.C.9). The ★ found after Standard 3 indicates that it is intended to be used to connect students' understanding of mathematical content with "physical, economic, public policy, social, and everyday situations" (CCSSI, 2010c, p. 72). This indication offers some insight into the types of problems that the writers intend students to solve when working with volume formulas for cylinders, pyramids, cones, and spheres.

Visualize relationships between two-dimensional and three-dimensional objects

The final, single-standard cluster in this domain (see Figure 5.14) builds on and formalizes students' understanding about cross-sections of three-dimensional objects, first addressed in 7th grade (7.G.A.3).

Figure 5.14 | **Visualize Relationships Between Two-Dimensional and Three-Dimensional Objects**

HSG-GMD.B

4. Identify the shapes of two-dimensional cross-sections of three-dimensional objects, and identify three-dimensional objects generated by rotations of two-dimensional objects.

Students may find it helpful to connect the idea of transformations, found in preceding Geometry domains, to the idea of generating a three-dimensional object. As explained in the Geometry introduction, students may benefit from the use of a dynamic geometry environment, as it will assist them in their investigations of geometric phenomena such as the rotation of two-dimensional objects.

Modeling with Geometry ★

All content within this final Geometry domain focuses on modeling, as reflected both in the domain title and in the ★ found after all three standards. This entire domain, then, is intended to help students learn to apply what they know about geometric concepts to solve problems in practical situations, as described in Mathematical Practice Standard 4, "Model with mathematics."

The ability to model with mathematics goes hand in hand with the ability to "reason abstractly and quantitatively" (Mathematical Practice Standard 2). The standards within this domain ask students not only to look at problem situations from the abstract (contextual) point of view but also to envision the same problem situation from the quantitative (mathematical) point of view. Similarly, as students reason about physical situations, such as the number of people in a square mile, the ability to reason from both perspectives will allow them to make sense of and solve the problem (Mathematical Practice Standard 1).

Modeling with Geometry has three standards in a single cluster.

Apply geometric concepts in modeling situations

As the name of this cluster implies, the work here has students deeply engaged in modeling practices (see Figure 5.15).

All three standards are marked with a ★, indicating that each is intended to help students understand how mathematics applies to "physical, economic, public policy, social, and everyday situations" (CCSSI, 2010c, p. 72). While working on any of these standards, students will be learning

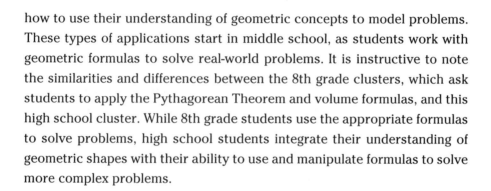

Figure 5.15 | **Apply Geometric Concepts in Modeling Situations**

1. Use geometric shapes, their measures, and their properties to describe objects (e.g., modeling a tree trunk or a human torso as a cylinder). ★
2. Apply concepts of density based on area and volume in modeling situations (e.g., persons per square mile, BTUs per cubic foot). ★
3. Apply geometric methods to solve design problems (e.g., designing an object or structure to satisfy physical constraints or minimize cost; working with typographic grid systems based on ratios). ★

how to use their understanding of geometric concepts to model problems. These types of applications start in middle school, as students work with geometric formulas to solve real-world problems. It is instructive to note the similarities and differences between the 8th grade clusters, which ask students to apply the Pythagorean Theorem and volume formulas, and this high school cluster. While 8th grade students use the appropriate formulas to solve problems, high school students integrate their understanding of geometric shapes with their ability to use and manipulate formulas to solve more complex problems.

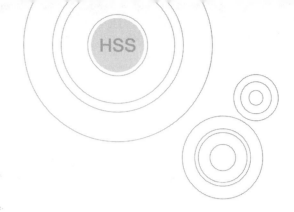

CHAPTER 6

Statistics and Probability

The final conceptual category in high school mathematics is Statistics and Probability (HSS), which is divided into four domains:

- Interpreting Categorical and Quantitative Data (HSS-ID)
- Making Inferences and Justifying Conclusions (HSS-IC)
- Conditional Probability and the Rules of Probability (HSS-CP)
- Using Probability to Make Decisions (HSS-MD)

The first two domains focus on data interpretation, and the second two focus on probability.

The concepts found in the Statistics and Probability conceptual category are intended to be integrated into all three traditional (or integrated) courses, given a slightly different focus to correspond to the other content addressed in each course. For example, Appendix A (CCSSI, 2010d) places the "Interpret linear models" cluster (HSS-ID.C) from the Interpreting Categorical and Quantitative Data domain in Algebra I (Integrated Mathematics I) because the statistics concepts in the cluster align instructionally with the algebra concepts in that course.

Now, let's examine the domains, clusters, and standards in more detail.

Interpreting Categorical and Quantitative Data

This domain is the first of two that focus on statistical data, emphasizing the mathematical tools needed to summarize, represent, and interpret data. As seen in Appendix A, the majority of the concepts found in this first domain are intended to be introduced in students' first year of high school (Algebra I or Mathematics I) and to serve as a foundation for the content found in the second domain, Making Inferences and Justifying Conclusions (see p. 86).

As students interpret statistical data, analyzing givens and relationships, they're engaging in activities related to Mathematical Practice Standard 1, "Make sense of problems and persevere in solving them." The ability to translate back and forth between data sets and problem contexts is evidence that students are reasoning abstractly and quantitatively (Mathematical Practice Standard 2) as well as modeling with mathematics (Mathematical Practice Standard 4). When students distinguish between correlation and causation, they're engaging with an important concept in the development of viable arguments (Mathematical Practice Standard 2) and learning to communicate their ideas precisely (Mathematical Practice Standard 6). The appropriate use of technological tools to assist with the generation of plots, regression functions, and correlation coefficients corresponds with Mathematical Practice Standard 5, "Use appropriate tools strategically."

The Interpeting Categorical and Quantitive Data domain has nine standards, organized into three clusters.

Summarize, represent, and interpret data on a single count or measurement variable

This first cluster (see Figure 6.1) builds on students' understanding of the graphing of data, which has been developed throughout the grades.

Students were first introduced to the representation and interpretation of data in elementary school when they were asked to make and interpret graphs and line plots to display data sets. By middle school, they had begun to analyze quantitative relationships between variables and to display numerical data on

Figure 6.1 | **Summarize, Represent, and Interpret Data on a Single Count or Measurement Variable**

1. Represent data with plots on the real number line (dot plots, histograms, and box plots).
2. Use statistics appropriate to the shape of the data distribution to compare center (median, mean) and spread (interquartile range, standard deviation) of two or more different data sets.
3. Interpret differences in shape, center, and spread in the context of the data sets, accounting for possible effects of extreme data points (outliers).
4. Use the mean and standard deviation of a data set to fit it to a normal distribution and to estimate population percentages. Recognize that there are data sets for which such a procedure is not appropriate. Use calculators, spreadsheets, and tables to estimate areas under the normal curve.

dot plots, histograms, and box plots (6.SP.B.4) and to summarize and describe distributions (6.SP.B.5). While the difference between the middle school and high school concepts is not immediately apparent from the standards, Appendix A gives some guidance about the writers' intentions, as follows:

> In grades 6–8, students describe center and spread in a data distribution. Here [high school mathematics] they choose a summary statistic appropriate to the characteristics of the data distribution, such as the shape of the distribution or the existence of extreme data points. (CCSSI, 2010d, p. 22)

Therefore, it is the student's reasoned choice of a summary statistic that differentiates the high school expectations from those of middle school.

Summarize, represent, and interpret data on two categorical and quantitative variables

The next cluster (see Figure 6.2) furthers students' understanding of the representation and interpretation of data.

Standards 5 (HSS-ID.B.5) and 6 (HSS-ID.B.6) extend students' understanding of the graphing of single-variable data to two numerical variables and

Figure 6.2 | **Summarize, Represent, and Interpret Data on Two Categorical and Quantitative Variables**

5. Summarize categorical data for two categories in two-way frequency tables. Interpret relative frequencies in the context of the data (including joint, marginal, and conditional relative frequencies). Recognize possible associations and trends in the data.

6. Represent data on two quantitative variables on a scatter plot, and describe how the variables are related.

    a. Fit a function to the data; use functions fitted to data to solve problems in the context of the data. *Use given functions or choose a function suggested by the context. Emphasize linear, quadratic, and exponential models.*

    b. Informally assess the fit of a function by plotting and analyzing residuals.

    c. Fit a linear function for a scatter plot that suggests a linear association.

adds scatter plots. This content is also found in 8th grade, where students are asked to construct and interpret scatter plots for bivariate measurement data (8.SP.A.1). Students are now asked to do a more complex analysis of a scatter plot, integrating the concept of linear, quadratic, and exponential functions. Students may find it useful to connect the content found in Functions regarding the application of functions in context (HSF-IF.B.4) to the fitting of a function to a scatter plot. In addition to addressing the fitting of a function, the "b" component of Standard 6 (HSS-ID.B.6b) asks that students analyze residuals to assess how well the model fits. Appendix A gives some guidance about the expectations for this section of the standard, explaining that while the primary focus should be on linear functions, this section could be used to allow students to preview quadratic functions as well.

Interpret linear models

In 8th grade, students learn to evaluate linear functions, including interpreting the slope of a given function in qualitative terms. This skill is further developed in the high school Functions category, when students are asked to calculate and interpret the rate of change of a function over a specified interval (HSF-IF.B.6) and to use technology to graph functions and show the intercepts (HSF-IF.C.7). This cluster (see Figure 6.3) builds on those

HSS-ID.C

Figure 6.3 ǀ **Interpret Linear Models**
7. Interpret the slope (rate of change) and the intercept (constant term) of a linear model in the context of the data.
8. Compute (using technology) and interpret the correlation coefficient of a linear fit.
9. Distinguish between correlation and causation.

skills, asking students to apply them in the context of a given data set in Standard 7 (HSS-ID.C.7) and to compute and interpret the correlation coefficient of a linear fit in Standard 8 (HSS-ID.C.8).

The important distinction between correlation and causation in Standard 9 (HSS-ID.C.9) will assist students as they learn how to make inferences and justify conclusions from sample surveys, experiments, and observational studies, which is the focus of the next domain.

Making Inferences and Justifying Conclusions

This domain is the second within the Statistics and Probability category to focus on data interpretation. While the first domain primarily addressed how to represent and interpret data, this one introduces the logical processes involved in making inferences and justifying conclusions from statistical experiments. As explained in Appendix A, the standards in this domain are intended to be integrated into a third-year mathematics course, as students begin to learn how to use the skills developed in earlier grades regarding data display and interpretation to make reasoned inferences about a given population. In addition, students will learn about the different methods of gathering data and the importance of the conditions under which the data were gathered.

As students interpret statistical data, they'll engage in activities related to Mathematical Practice Standard 1, such as analyzing givens and relationships to make sense of problems. The ability to translate back and forth between data sets and problem contexts is evidence that students are reasoning abstractly and quantitatively (Mathematical Practice Standard 2) and modeling with mathematics (Mathematical Practice Standard 4). When students justify conclusions from sample surveys, experiments, and observational studies, they are working to develop viable arguments (Mathematical Practice Standard 2) and communicate their ideas precisely (Mathematical Practice Standard 6).

This domain has six standards, grouped in two clusters.

Understand and evaluate random processes underlying statistical experiments

Students should already be familiar with the foundational ideas of population parameters and random sampling found in this cluster (see Figure 6.4), as both concepts are addressed in 7th grade (7.SP.A, 7.SP.B). These standards in the middle school Statistics and Probability domain ask students to understand and use random sampling of a population as a way of drawing inferences about a population. The ideas are revisited in high school via this domain's Standards 1 and 2 (HSS-IC.A.1–2), which also provide a new focus on evaluating the methodology of the experiment.

Figure 6.4 | **Understand and Evaluate Random Processes Underlying Statistical Experiments**

1. Understand statistics as a process for making inferences about population parameters based on a random sample from that population.
2. Decide if a specified model is consistent with results from a given data-generating process, e.g., using simulation. *For example, a model says a spinning coin falls heads up with probability 0.5. Would a result of 5 tails in a row cause you to question the model?*

Make inferences and justify conclusions from sample surveys, experiments, and observational studies

The standards in this cluster (see Figure 6.5) call on students to apply the understanding of random sampling they developed through their work on Standards HSS-IC.A.1–2.

HSS-IC.B

Figure 6.5 | **Make Inferences and Justify Conclusions from Sample Surveys, Experiments, and Observational Studies**

3. Recognize the purposes of and differences among sample surveys, experiments, and observational studies; explain how randomization relates to each.
4. Use data from a sample survey to estimate a population mean or proportion; develop a margin of error through the use of simulation models for random sampling.
5. Use data from a randomized experiment to compare two treatments; use simulations to decide if differences between parameters are significant.
6. Evaluate reports based on data.

While they are engaged in sample surveys, experiments, and observational studies, students will find it useful to draw upon the foundational conceptions of population parameters and random sampling described in the previous cluster and in the 7th grade statistics and probability standards (7.SP.A, 7.SP.B). As described in Appendix A, students, by drawing upon this understanding, can begin to focus on the differences between types of data collection as well as on how data collection processes can alter the scope and nature of the conclusions reached from the data. The resulting understandings may be helpful to students as they continue on in courses requiring research, including physical science, the social sciences, and advanced mathematics courses.

Conditional Probability and the Rules of Probability

The first two domains in the Statistics and Probability category focus on statistical data analysis, making this one the first to focus on probability. According to Appendix A, the study of probability should occur in Geometry (Mathematics II). Because this content is designed to be taught in second-year math, Appendix A urges students to make use of geometric probability models "wherever possible," thereby connecting some of the concepts in Geometry to the ideas found in this domain (CCSSI, 2010d, p. 68).

Although students encounter topics in descriptive statistics in 8th grade mathematics (8.SP.A) and in Algebra I or Mathematics I, most will have had few formal learning experiences with probability after 7th grade mathematics. Prior to the adoption of the Common Core standards, this material was commonly found in college readiness standards but not something all students were required to study.

Working in this domain, students will interpret data using the concepts of independence and conditional probability and will engage in activities such as analyzing givens and relationships. These practices align with Mathematical Practice Standard 1. As students translate back and forth between data sets and problem contexts, they show evidence that they are reasoning abstractly and quantitatively (Mathematical Practice Standard 2) and modeling with mathematics (Mathematical Practice Standard 4). When students work to apply the rules of probability to compute probabilities or compound events, they may find themselves needing to step back at times and shift perspective, so that they can see the more complicated rules and data sets both as single objects and as being composed of several objects. Being able to shift perspective is an ability associated with Mathematical Practice Standard 7, "Look for and make use of structure."

> For an example of a Geometry or Mathematics II lesson addressing three standards in this domain (HSS-CP.A.4, HSS-CP.A.5, and HSS-CP.B.6) see **Sample Lesson 2**.

This domain has nine standards, organized into two clusters.

Understand independence and conditional probability and use them to interpret data

According to Appendix A of the standards document, the content in this cluster (see Figure 6.6) is designed to be taught in second-year high school math (Geometry or Mathematics II).

Students are introduced to aspects of probability in grade 7, when they are asked to develop, use, and evaluate probability models (7.SP.C). Appendix A notes that the content in this cluster builds on that foundation, developing the more complex ideas around set theory that allow students "to expand their ability to compute and interpret theoretical

Figure 6.6 | **Understand Independence and Conditional Probability and Use Them to Interpret Data**

1. Describe events as subsets of a sample space (the set of outcomes) using characteristics (or categories) of the outcomes, or as unions, intersections, or complements of other events ("or," "and," "not").
2. Understand that two events *A* and *B* are independent if the probability of *A* and *B* occurring together is the product of their probabilities, and use this characterization to determine if they are independent.
3. Understand the conditional probability of *A* given *B* as *P*(*A* and *B*)/*P*(*B*), and interpret independence of *A* and *B* as saying that the conditional probability of *A* given *B* is the same as the probability of *A*, and the conditional probability of *B* given *A* is the same as the probability of *B*.
4. Construct and interpret two-way frequency tables of data when two categories are associated with each object being classified. Use the two-way table as a sample space to decide if events are independent and to approximate conditional probabilities. *For example, collect data from a random sample of students in your school on their favorite subject among math, science, and English. Estimate the probability that a randomly selected student from your school will favor science given that the student is in 10th grade. Do the same for other subjects and compare the results.*
5. Recognize and explain the concepts of conditional probability and independence in everyday language and everyday situations. *For example, compare the chance of having lung cancer if you are a smoker with the chance of being a smoker if you have lung cancer.*

and experimental probabilities for compound events" (CCSSI, 2010d, p. 35). Within this cluster, Standard 4 (HSS-CP.A.4) also draws on the work with two-way tables from the Interpreting Categorical and Quantitative Data domain, which is designed to be taught in first-year high school mathematics (Algebra I or Mathematics I).

Use the rules of probability to compute probabilities of compound events in a uniform probability model

The content in Cluster B (see Figure 6.7) is also intended for second-year high school math, during which students begin to develop more complex ideas around set theory. Standards 6–9 (HSS-CP.B.6–9) will continue that development, as students begin to use the rules of probability.

Figure 6.7 | Use the Rules of Probability to Compute Probabilities of Compound Events in a Uniform Probability Model

6. Find the conditional probability of A given B as the fraction of B's outcomes that also belong to A, and interpret the answer in terms of the model.

7. Apply the Addition Rule, $P(A \text{ or } B) = P(A) + P(B) - P(A \text{ and } B)$, and interpret the answer in terms of the model.

8. (+) Apply the general Multiplication Rule in a uniform probability model, $P(A \text{ and } B) = P(A)P(B|A) = P(B)P(A|B)$, and interpret the answer in terms of the model.

9. (+) Use permutations and combinations to compute probabilities of compound events and solve problems.

The last two standards in this cluster, Standard 8 (HSS-CP.B.8) and Standard 9 (HSS-CP.B.9), are marked with a (+), indicating that the Multiplication Rule and permutations and combinations are considered advanced topics. Appendix A lists them as optional standards for Geometry or Mathematics II. The content they cover flows logically from the other standards in Cluster B, and it should be accessible to students after they have mastered the first seven standards in the Conditional Probability and the Rules of Probability domain. Even so, because Standards 8 and 9 are not required of all students, they might remain unaddressed if limited instructional time is a factor.

Using Probability to Make Decisions

While the previous domain addressed probability by extending students' understanding from their middle school foundation in conditional probability and focused on the rules of probability, the final domain in the Statistics and Probability category gives students tools that allow for the interpretation of probability distributions.

All standards in this domain are marked with a (+), indicating that using probability to make decisions is considered an advanced topic that will not be required of all students. Despite that designation, Appendix A includes two of the standards in the final cluster of the domain ("Use probability to evaluate outcomes of decisions") as optional content in second- and third-year high school mathematics courses, which may be a result of the perceived relative accessibility of these standards.

Working under this domain, students will engage in activities such as analyzing decision strategies using probability contexts, thereby making sense of problems and addressing Mathematical Practice Standard 1. The ability to translate back and forth between data sets and problem contexts is evidence that students are reasoning abstractly and quantitatively (Mathematical Practice Standard 2) and modeling with mathematics (Mathematical Practice Standard 4).

The Using Probability to Make Decisions domain contains seven standards, grouped in two clusters.

Calculate expected values and use them to solve problems

The content within Cluster A (see Figure 6.8) will help students develop a deeper understanding of the use of statistical data, which will help them both in courses requiring research projects and in solving real-life problems.

HSS-MD.A

Figure 6.8 | **Calculate Expected Values and Use Them to Solve Problems**

1. (+) Define a random variable for a quantity of interest by assigning a numerical value to each event in a sample space; graph the corresponding probability distribution using the same graphical displays as for data distributions.
2. (+) Calculate the expected value of a random variable; interpret it as the mean of the probability distribution.
3. (+) Develop a probability distribution for a random variable defined for a sample space in which theoretical probabilities can be calculated; find the expected value. *For example, find the theoretical probability distribution for the number of correct answers obtained by guessing on all five questions of a multiple-choice test where each question has four choices, and find the expected grade under various grading schemes.*
4. (+) Develop a probability distribution for a random variable defined for a sample space in which probabilities are assigned empirically; find the expected value. *For example, find a current data distribution on the number of TV sets per household in the United States, and calculate the expected number of sets per household. How many TV sets would you expect to find in 100 randomly selected households?*

According to Appendix A, this material is designed to be taught in a fourth-year course to prepare students for advanced mathematics. It will logically build on the probability concepts found in the Conditional Probability and the Rules of Probability domain, which Appendix A places in a second-year math course. Standards 1–4 (HSS-MD.A.1–4) also build on the concepts found in the Statistics and Probability category's first and second domains (Interpreting Categorical and Quantitative Data, Making Inferences and Justifying Conclusions) regarding the importance of randomness and the use of data distributions.

Use probability to evaluate outcomes of decisions

While the first cluster focuses on the calculation of expected values and the development of probability distributions for random variables, this cluster (see Figure 6.9) centers on using that understanding to evaluate the outcomes of decisions.

Figure 6.9 | **Use Probability to Evaluate Outcomes of Decisions**

5. (+) Weigh the possible outcomes of a decision by assigning probabilities to payoff values and finding expected values.
   a. Find the expected payoff for a game of chance. *For example, find the expected winnings from a state lottery ticket or a game at a fast-food restaurant.*
   b. Evaluate and compare strategies on the basis of expected values. *For example, compare a high-deductible versus a low-deductible automobile insurance policy using various, but reasonable, chances of having a minor or a major accident.*
6. (+) Use probabilities to make fair decisions (e.g., drawing by lots, using a random number generator).
7. (+) Analyze decisions and strategies using probability concepts (e.g., product testing, medical testing, pulling a hockey goalie at the end of a game).

The three standards here, like all others in the domain, are marked with a (+), indicating that the use of probability concepts to evaluate the outcomes of decisions is considered an advanced topic not required of all students. According to Appendix A, while Standard 5 (HSS-MD.B.5) is designed to be taught in a fourth-year course to prepare students for advanced mathematics, Standard 6 (HSS-MD.B.6) and Standard 7 (HSS-MD.B.7) are placed in the second and third years of high school mathematics. This placement may be due to these standards' perceived lower level of difficulty or to the fact that Standard 6 and Standard 7 integrate well with the probability content found in the Conditional Probability and the Rules of Probability domain. The content within this cluster will help students to develop a deeper understanding of the use of statistical data and aid them both in courses requiring research projects and in addressing real-life problems.

CHAPTER 7

Guidance for Instructional Planning

In this chapter, we provide a brief tutorial on designing lesson plans using the types of instructional strategies that appear in this guide's sample lessons. It includes a step-by-step outline for the development of lessons that make best use of proven instructional strategies and will help you ensure students master the new and challenging content represented by the Common Core standards.

The Framework for Instructional Planning

To identify and use effective strategies to develop these lessons, we draw on the instructional planning framework developed for *Classroom Instruction That Works, 2nd edition* (Dean et al., 2012), presented in Figure 7.1.

The Framework organizes nine categories of research-based strategies for increasing student achievement into three components. These components focus on three key aspects of teaching and learning: creating an environment for learning, helping students develop understanding, and helping students extend and apply knowledge. Let's take a close look at each.

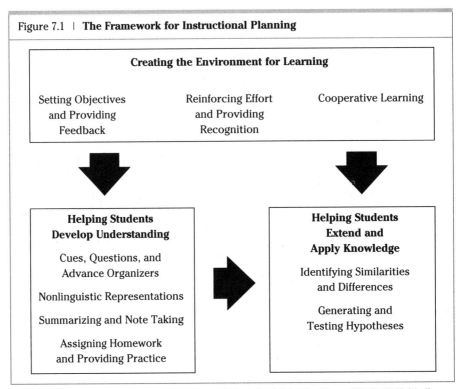

Figure 7.1 | **The Framework for Instructional Planning**

Creating the Environment for Learning

Setting Objectives and Providing Feedback

Reinforcing Effort and Providing Recognition

Cooperative Learning

Helping Students Develop Understanding

Cues, Questions, and Advance Organizers

Nonlinguistic Representations

Summarizing and Note Taking

Assigning Homework and Providing Practice

Helping Students Extend and Apply Knowledge

Identifying Similarities and Differences

Generating and Testing Hypotheses

Source: From *Classroom Instruction That Works, 2nd ed.* (p. xvi) by Ceri Dean, Elizabeth Hubbell, Howard Pitler, and Bj Stone, 2012, Alexandria, VA: ASCD; and Denver, CO: McREL. Copyright 2012 by McREL. Adapted with permission.

Creating the environment for learning

Teachers create a positive environment for learning when they ensure that students are motivated and focused, know what's expected of them, and regularly receive feedback on their progress. When the environment is right, students are actively engaged in their learning and have multiple opportunities to share and discuss ideas with their peers.

A number of instructional strategies that help create a positive environment for learning may be incorporated into the lesson design itself. Other aspects, such as reinforcing effort and providing recognition, may not be a formal part of the lesson plan but are equally important. The following strategies are essential for creating a positive environment for learning:

- Setting objectives and providing feedback
- Reinforcing effort and providing recognition
- Cooperative learning

Helping students develop understanding

This component of the Framework focuses on strategies that are designed to help students work with what they already know and help them integrate new content with their prior understanding. To ensure that students study effectively outside class, teachers also need strategies that support constructive approaches to assigning homework. The strategies that help students develop understanding include the following:

- Cues, questions, and advance organizers
- Nonlinguistic representations
- Summarizing and note taking
- Assigning homework and providing practice

Helping students extend and apply knowledge

In this component of the Framework, teachers use strategies that prompt students to move beyond the "right answers," engage in more complex reasoning, and consider the real-world connections and applications of targeted content and skills, all of which help students gain flexibility when it comes to using what they have learned. The following strategies help students extend and apply knowledge:

- Identifying similarities and differences
- Generating and testing hypotheses

Figure 7.2 illustrates the three major components of teaching and learning described in *Classroom Instruction That Works*, along with the nine types, or categories, of strategies that further define the components and point you toward activities that will suit your learning objectives and support your students' success.

Component	Category	Definition
Figure 7.2 | Framework Components and the Associated Categories of Instructional Strategies		
Creating the Environment for Learning	Setting Objectives and Providing Feedback	Provide students with a direction for learning and with information about how well they are performing relative to a particular learning objective so they can improve their performance.
	Reinforcing Effort and Providing Recognition	Enhance students' understanding of the relationship between effort and achievement by addressing students' attitudes and beliefs about learning. Provide students with non-material tokens of recognition or praise for their accomplishments related to the attainment of a goal.
	Cooperative Learning	Provide students with opportunities to interact with one another in ways that enhance their learning.
Helping Students Develop Understanding	Cues, Questions, and Advance Organizers	Enhance students' ability to retrieve, use, and organize what they already know about a topic.
	Nonlinguistic Representations • Graphic Organizers • Pictures and Pictographs • Mental Images • Kinesthetic Movement • Models/Manipulatives	Enhance students' ability to represent and elaborate on knowledge using mental images.
	Summarizing and Note Taking	Enhance students' ability to synthesize information and organize it in a way that captures the main ideas and supporting details.
	Providing Practice, and Assigning Homework	Extend the learning opportunities for students to practice, review, and apply knowledge. Enhance students' ability to reach the expected level of proficiency for a skill or process

Component	Category	Definition
Figure 7.2 **Framework Components and the Associated Categories of Instructional Strategies** *(continued)*		
Helping Students Extend and Apply Knowledge	Identifying Similarities and Differences • Comparing • Classifying • Creating/Using Metaphors • Creating/Using Analogies	Enhance students' understanding of and ability to use knowledge by engaging them in mental processes that involve identifying ways in which items are alike and different.
	Generating and Testing Hypotheses	Enhance students' understanding of and ability to use knowledge by engaging them in mental processes that involve making and testing hypotheses.

Source: From *Classroom Instruction That Works, 2nd ed.* (p. xviii) by Ceri Dean, Elizabeth Hubbell, Howard Pitler, and Bj Stone, 2012, Alexandria, VA: ASCD; and Denver, CO: McREL. Copyright 2012 by McREL. Adapted with permission.

Lesson Development, Step by Step

To help you get started developing lessons that incorporate these strategies, we provide a step-by-step process to ensure that you've had an opportunity to consider where within a lesson the various strategies might be used most effectively. Those steps are as follows:

1. Identify the focus for the lesson.
2. Determine how learning will be assessed.
3. Determine the activities that will start the lesson.
4. Determine the activities that will engage students in learning the content.
5. Determine the activities that will close the lesson.

Let's look now at the details of each step and how you might incorporate the nine effective instructional strategies associated with each of the Framework's three components. We'll reference the sample lessons in this guide to illustrate particular aspects of this approach.

Step 1: Identify the focus for the lesson

The critical first step in crafting a lesson is to identify what students should learn as a result of their engagement in the lesson activities. Setting objectives for students also means establishing the guidelines for your development of the lesson: namely, that you will select and develop only those activities that will help students meet the objectives set. A learning objective is built directly from a standard; the objectives found in this guide's sample lessons are constructed from Common Core standards and listed under the heading "Common Core State Standards—Knowledge and Skills to Be Addressed."

Clarifying learning objectives. To ensure that students are clear about what they will learn, you will want your lesson plans to include more specific statements of the objectives in clear, student-friendly language. Some teachers accomplish this by using stems such as "I can . . ." or "We will be able to . . ." or "Students will be able to . . ." and providing a paraphrased version of the standard, simplifying the language as necessary. In the sample lessons for this guide, such specifics may be found under the headings "Knowledge/Vocabulary Objectives" and "Skill/Process Objectives" and prefaced by either "Students will understand . . ." or "Students will be able to. . . ."

Identifying essential questions and learning objectives. Framing the lesson's objectives under a broader essential question provides students with alternate avenues to find personal relevance and can energize them to seek answers as they begin a unit or lesson. The essential question properly focuses on the broader purpose of learning, and it is most effective when it is open-ended and not a question that can be easily answered. Each of the sample lessons includes an essential question—the learning objectives reframed to clarify for students what value the lesson holds for them.

Identifying foundational knowledge and possible misconceptions related to the learning objectives. As you develop learning objectives for a lesson, consider the other skills students will need to use but that will not be the explicit focus of instruction or assessment. Our discussions of each standard in this guide identify the critical knowledge and skills that students are assumed to have mastered or practiced in lessons prior to learning the new content. In the sample lessons, you'll find these standards under the heading "Common Core State Standards—Prior Knowledge and Skills to Be Applied."

Step 2: Determine how learning will be assessed

As important as identifying the learning objective for a lesson is identifying the criteria you will use to determine if students have met that objective. You will want to be clear about the rigor identified in the Common Core standards. As you develop scoring tools, such as checklists, and rubrics that define the various levels of performance related to the objective's knowledge or skill, it is important to review the details of the objective's underlying standard to be sure you are looking for the appropriate level of mastery.

Assessing prior knowledge. Step 2 involves planning how to measure students' prior knowledge, especially the knowledge identified in Step 1 as prerequisite to mastery of the learning objective. For example, you might ask students to complete a short problem or share reflections on their prior experiences with similar tasks. This approach may also surface any lingering student misconceptions that you'll want to address before proceeding.

Providing feedback. This part of the planning process also includes deciding how you will provide students with feedback on their progress toward the outcome. Providing feedback is an important aspect of creating the environment for learning because understanding what good performance looks like, how to judge their own performance relative to a benchmark, and what they need to do to improve their performance helps students develop a sense of control over their learning. During lesson planning, you might also consider how peers can give their classmates feedback on progress toward the stated objective.

Step 3: Determine the activities that will start the lesson

Step 3 of the planning process concerns the sequence of activities at the start of the lesson, which relate to the "Creating the Environment for Learning" component of the Framework for Instructional Planning. The beginning of each lesson should be orchestrated to capture students' interest, communicate the learning objectives, and encourage their commitment to effort.

Communicating learning objectives. You can share learning objectives by stating them orally, but be sure to post them in writing for reference throughout the lesson. Doing so not only reminds the class of the objectives' importance but also ensures that even students who weren't paying close attention or who came in late can identify what they are working to achieve.

Identifying the essential question and providing a context. Students engage in learning more readily when they can see how it connects to their own interests. The essential question you provide at the beginning of the lesson helps orient them to the purpose for learning. Students will also have a greater sense of involvement if you share with them what activities they'll be engaged in and how these activities will help build their understanding and skill. The sample lessons in this guide present this preview under the heading "Activity Description to Share with Students." It is something you might read aloud or post, along with the objectives and essential questions, as you create the environment for learning at the beginning of a lesson. To encourage greater involvement, you might also ask students to set personal goals based on the learning objectives in each activity. These personal goals may translate the learning objective to immediate goals that resonate for each student.

Reinforcing effort. As you develop the activities for the lesson, look for natural points where you might build in opportunities for students to receive encouragement they need to continue their work. To reinforce student effort, we need to help students understand the direct connection between how hard they work and what they achieve. It's another way in which teachers can provide students with a greater sense of control over their own learning.

Step 4: Determine the activities that will engage students in learning the content

At Step 4 we are at the crux of the lesson, deciding what students will do to acquire, extend, and apply knowledge or skills. This stage of planning includes identifying when formative assessment should take place, when you will provide students feedback from the assessment, and how you will ensure that students have a clear understanding of how they are doing. And, of course, you will need to decide which instructional activities will best serve the lesson's primary purposes, considering whether the activities need to focus on helping students acquire new knowledge and skill or extend and refine what they've already learned.

Choosing activities and strategies that develop student understanding. When your aim is to help students understand new information or a new process, then you will want to design activities that incorporate strategies associated with that component of the Framework for Instructional Planning. These are the strategies that help students access prior knowledge and organize new learning. Students come to every lesson with some prior knowledge, and the effective use of strategies such as using cues, questions, and advance organizers can enhance students' ability to retrieve and use what they already know about a topic in order to access something new. You can help students access and leverage their prior knowledge through simple discussion, by providing "KWL"-type advance organizers, by having students read or listen to short texts related to the targeted content, or any of a number of ways. Activities incorporating the use of nonlinguistic representations (including visualization) in which students elaborate on knowledge, skills, and processes are other good ways to help students integrate new learning into existing knowledge. The strategies of note taking and summarizing also support students' efforts to synthesize information through the act of organizing it in a way that captures its main ideas and supporting details or highlights key aspects of new processes. Finally, homework can help students learn or review new content and practice skills so that they can more quickly reach the expected level of proficiency. However, you will want to think carefully about your homework practices, as the research on what makes homework effective shows mixed results. Dean and colleagues (2012) recommend that teachers design homework assignments that directly support learning objectives. Students need to understand how homework serves lesson objectives, and once homework is completed, it is important that teachers provide feedback on the assignment.

Choosing activities and strategies that help students extend and apply knowledge. When your aim is to help students extend or apply their knowledge or master skills and processes, they will need opportunities to practice independently. What are beneficial are activities that involve making comparisons, classifying, and creating or using metaphors and analogies. Research summarized in the second edition of *Classroom Instruction That Works* indicates that these strategies, associated with the "Helping Students Extend and Apply Knowledge" component of the Framework for Instructional Planning, are a worthwhile use of instructional time. They help to raise students' levels of understanding and improve their ability to use what they learn. Because students need to understand the concepts or skills that they're comparing, you are more likely to insert these activities later in a lesson than at the outset.

Remember, too, that strategies that help students generate and test hypotheses are not meant just for science classrooms. They are a way to deepen students' knowledge by requiring them to use critical-thinking skills, such as analysis and evaluation.

Grouping students for activities. Cooperative learning can be tremendously beneficial, whether students are developing a new skill or understanding or applying or extending it. With every lesson you design, consider when it makes sense to use this strategy, what kind of student grouping will be most beneficial, and how these groups should be composed. Cooperative learning is a strong option, for example, when you want to differentiate an activity based on student readiness, interest, or learning style. Consider, too, that students' learning experiences will be different depending on whether you permit them to self-select into groups of their choosing or assign their group partners, whether the groups are larger (four or five students) or smaller (e.g., pair work), and whether these groups are homogeneous or heterogeneous.

Providing students with the opportunity to share and discuss their ideas with one another in varying cooperative learning arrangements lays a foundation for the world beyond school, which depends on people working interdependently to solve problems and to innovate. Interacting with one another also deepens students' knowledge of the concepts they are learning; in other words, talking about ideas and listening to others' ideas helps students understand a topic and retain what they've learned, and it may send their thinking in interesting new directions.

Step 5: Determine the activities that will close the lesson

Bringing the lesson to a close provides an opportunity for you and students to look back on and sum up the learning experience.

During this part of the lesson, you want to return to the learning objectives and confirm that you have addressed each of them. This can be approached in one or more ways—through informal sharing, formative assessment, or even summative assessment. Students benefit from the opportunity to gauge their progress in learning. You might prompt them to reflect on the lesson in a journal entry, learning log, or response card, which can easily serve as an informal check for understanding. Note that asking students to share what they found most difficult as well as what worked well can provide you with insight you can apply during the next lesson and can use to refine the lesson just completed.

Depending upon the nature of the objective and whether the lesson appears late in the unit, you may elect to conduct a formal summative assessment. Alternatively, you may identify a homework assignment tied to the learning objective, making sure that students understand how the assignment will help them deepen their understanding or develop their skill.

* * *

In the remaining pages of this guide, we offer sample lesson plans based on the Common Core State Standards for Mathematics, the Framework for Instructional Planning, and the steps just outlined.

Growth Models—Connecting Linear and Exponential Functions

Course: Algebra I or Integrated Pathway: Mathematics I
Length of Lesson: One hour; one 60-minute class period

Introduction

In grade 8, students build a foundation for both linear and nonlinear functions, but as students begin high school courses, they are asked to recognize functions as larger algebraic structures that possess certain characteristics and behave in certain ways. In students' initial high school mathematics course, it is recommended that they investigate a variety of situations modeled by functions. In one model mathematics course pathway delineated in Appendix A of the Common Core mathematics standards, linear and exponential relationships are paired and taught within the first semester of the school year. While this may not be a traditional pairing of topics in an initial high school course, it can help students make connections between these concepts that will support the development of a deeper understanding.

This lesson is designed to provide students with a frame and process for building connections between linear and exponential relationships. To refine and cement this understanding, students will need additional problems and practice.

Strategies from the Framework for Instructional Planning

- *Creating the Environment for Learning:* The essential question ("How can growth be represented mathematically?") and learning objective ("To build an understanding of exponential function and how it can be modeled") are both central to the lesson. The teacher gives feedback throughout the lesson, and students give feedback to one another. Cooperative learning takes place with informal partnering and small groups as students make connections between the various representations of growth. The teacher uses relevant contexts to help students see mathematics in the world around them.
- *Helping Students Develop Understanding:* The lesson builds on prior knowledge about linear functions to help students understand exponential growth. Students use non-linguistic representations (graphs and tables) to build connections with the symbolic representation (the equation) as well as to build understanding of how exponential growth differs from linear growth. Additionally, the questions in the lesson require students to use analytical thinking, summarize, and make generalizations.
- *Helping Students Extend and Apply Knowledge:* Students are asked to look for similarities and differences between linear models and exponential models and to make predictions.

Common Core State Standards—Knowledge and Skills to Be Addressed

Standards for Mathematical Practice

MP4 Model with mathematics.

MP7 Look for and make use of structure.

MP8 Look for and express regularity in repeated reasoning.

Standards for Mathematical Content

Conceptual Category/Domain: Functions—Interpreting Functions

Cluster: Interpret Functions That Arise in Applications in Terms of the Context

HSF-IF.B.4 For a function that models a relationship between two quantities, interpret key features of graphs and tables in terms of the quantities, and sketch graphs showing key features given a verbal description of the relationship. *Key features include: intercepts; intervals where the function is increasing, decreasing, positive, or negative; relative maximums and minimums; symmetries; end behavior; and periodicity.*

Cluster: Analyze Functions Using Different Representations
HSF-IC.C.7 Graph functions expressed symbolically and show key features of the graph, by hand in simple cases and using technology for more complicated cases.

Common Core State Standards—Prior Knowledge and Skills to Be Applied

Domain: Expressions and Equations

Cluster: Work with Radicals and Integer Exponents
8.EE.A.1 Know and apply the properties of integer exponents to generate equivalent numerical expressions. *For example, $3^2 \times 3^{-5} = 3^{-3} = 1/3^3 = 1/27$.*

Domain: Functions

Cluster: Define, Evaluate, and Compare Functions
8.F.A.1 Understand that a function is a rule that assigns to each input exactly one output. The graph of a function is the set of ordered pairs consisting of an input and the corresponding output.
8.F.A.2 Compare properties of two functions each represented in a different way (algebraically, graphically, numerically in tables, or by verbal descriptions).
8.F.A.3 Interpret the equation $y = mx + b$ as defining a linear function, whose graph is a straight line; give examples of functions that are not linear.

Cluster: Use Functions to Model Relationships Between Quantities
8.F.B.5 Describe qualitatively the functional relationship between two quantities by analyzing a graph (e.g., where the function is increasing or decreasing, linear or nonlinear). Sketch a graph that exhibits the qualitative features of a function that has been described verbally.

Conceptual Category/Domain: Functions—Interpreting Functions

Cluster: Understand the Concept of a Function and Use Function Notation
HSF-IF.A.1 Understand that a function from one set (called the domain) to another set (called the range) assigns to each element of the domain exactly one element of the range. If f is a function and x is an element of its domain, then $f(x)$ denotes the output of f corresponding to the input x. The graph of f is the graph of the equation $y = f(x)$.

Teacher's Lesson Summary

This lesson focuses on comparing characteristics of linear and exponential functions that model growth. According to the National Research Council Committee on How People Learn (2005), students must connect prior learning to new concepts in order for real learning to occur, so it is important to intentionally make connections and distinctions between linear functions (prior learning) and exponential functions (new learning). Providing good questions and having students explain their reasoning will help the teacher better assess if students are grasping the concepts and skills.

Students will work in pairs or triads to investigate a variety of linear and exponential plots. As they move through the examples and questions, students will build an understanding of the characteristics of these representations and begin to make generalizations. Interactions with students during this work should include questions that bring students back to structure and repeated reasoning. The small-group assignment is designed to reinforce the set of mathematical practice standards associated with this lesson, listed on page 108.

Essential Question: How can growth be represented mathematically?
Learning Objective: To build an understanding of exponential function and how it can be modeled.

Knowledge/Vocabulary Objectives

At the conclusion of this lesson, students will

- Understand that linear and exponential functions represent growth models.
- Understand the features of an exponential graph in the form of $f(x) = b^x$ to include intercepts, intervals where the function is increasing or decreasing, and end behavior.
- Understand that exponential functions represent a percent rate of change in growth rather than a constant rate of change (linear).

Skill/Process Objectives

At the conclusion of this lesson, students will be able to

- Analyze exponential functions using different representations to include tables, graphs, symbolic notation, and verbal description.

- Predict changes in the graph based on changes to one variable.
- Compare similarities and differences of linear and exponential functions.
- Interpret functions that arise in applications in terms of the context.

Resources/Preparation Needed

- A problem set for the cooperative learning investigation of linear and exponential factors (see Figure A, pp. 117–118), one per group

Activity Description to Share with Students

Have you ever wondered how growth is modeled in mathematics? A person's earnings may increase (grow) as the number of hours worked increases. Or profit from a charity event may rise according to the number of tickets sold. But what type of growth describes how a virus spreads? Describes the change in intensity from an earthquake measuring 6 on the Richter scale to one measuring 7? This activity will help you visualize growth through various models and help you make connections between linear and exponential functions.

Lesson Activity Sequence

Start the Lesson

1. Post and discuss the essential question and learning objective. Share with students that they will be investigating exponential functions and they will start by using what they know about linear functions. Provide the following situation and ask student pairs to develop a response:

   > Suppose the student council is selling tickets for the senior class comedy show. Admission costs $5 per student, and all proceeds will go to the scholarship fund. How might you represent this scenario mathematically?

2. Allow student pairs a minute or two to discuss their responses, and then bring the class back together as a group. Prompt students to discuss the scenario as a model of linear growth. Questions such as the following might be helpful:

   - How could this information be displayed in a data table?
   - What is growing?

- What shape would the plot take?
- What equation could you use to represent this situation?
- How could the rate of change be described?

As a whole class, devise a list of characteristics of linear growth and keep this posted in the classroom for reference.

3. Ask students to think about how information spreads, using the following story or a similar one:

> Suppose one student learns an interesting bit of news and texts that news to two friends. These two friends each send a text to two more friends. Next, those two friends each text two friends, and so on.

Use a visual such as the following to help clarify the scenario. You may wish to add labels during the discussion to demonstrate the number of times the news was texted and how many people have heard it.

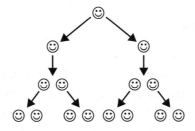

Ask: How might this growth scenario be represented on a plot?

4. Allow students to discuss this question in pairs for a minute or two, and then ask for predictions. Encourage discussion about how many students would know the story at the end of the fourth repetition, the fifth repetition, and so on.

5. Provide the plots shown at the top of page 113, and ask students to explain which of the plots best models the growth in the scenario you've been discussing. At this point, the shape of the plot is the primary point of focus.

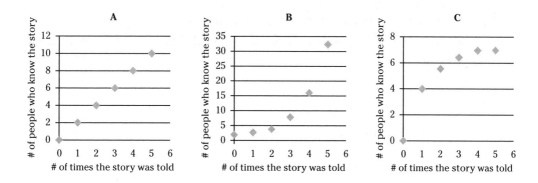

6. Help students understand that Plot B, an example of exponential growth, represents the texting situation. During the rest of the class, students will work to develop an understanding of exponential growth by building on their knowledge of linear growth.

Engage Students in Learning the Content

1. Ask students to take out a piece of notebook paper and predict the number of times that it can be folded. Additionally, ask them to think about how folding the piece of notebook paper will change its thickness. (For example, if a single, unfolded piece of paper is approximately 1 millimeter thick, how thick will it be when the maximum number of folds have been completed?) Allow students a minute or two to make and discuss their predictions, and then ask them to test these predictions by folding their piece of notebook paper as many times as they can, recording the number of resulting sections (i.e., no folds results in one section; one fold results in two sections, or halves; two folds results in four sections, or quarters; and so on) in a table and using the pattern that emerges to generate an algebraic representation for the paper-folding experiment:

x Number of folds	0	1	2	3				
y Number of sections	1	2						

Express *y* in terms of *x*: $y = ?$

2. Next ask students to compare the representation for the paper-folding experiment to the table below, which shows the sale of tickets at the senior class comedy show:

x Number of tickets sold	0	1	2	3				
y Dollars earned for ticket sales	0	5	10					

Express y in terms of x: $y = ?$

3. Help students make connections between the constant rate of change shown in the ticket sales scenario and the percent of change shown in the paper-folding experiment. Also prompt them to compare the thickness of the single sheet of paper to the thickness of the paper when the maximum number of folds have been made. It is the "suddenness" of exponential growth (increasing and decreasing) that is so mind-blowing.

4. Next share the following scenario, which illustrates a decreasing exponential plot:

> The NCAA basketball tournament traditionally begins with a field of 64 teams. When a team loses a game, that team is out of the tournament. At the end of round one (that is, after all teams have played one game), how many teams remain in the tournament?

Construct a table to show how many teams remain after each round of the tournament; then, plot the data, as shown at the top of page 115.

x Rounds of tournament play	0	1						
y # of teams remaining AFTER each round	64	32						

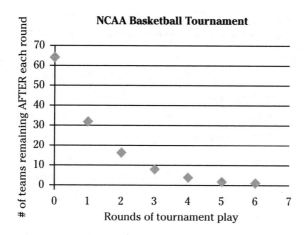

5. To gather the necessary data, engage the whole class in discussion, using prompting questions such as the following:

   • How does the number of teams left in each round compare to the number of teams in the previous round?

   • How many rounds are played in the tournament?

   • Does the plot represent a linear function? Explain your response.

   • How does this plot compare to the plot illustrating the texting scenario (Plot B)?

   • What happens as the graph approaches the *x*-axis? (Note: Discuss the term "end behavior.")

6. Assign students to pairs or groups of three and ask them to work cooperatively on the **Investigating Linear and Exponential Functions Problem Set** (see **Figure A**, pp. 117–118). Remind students that each small group will be asked to contribute to a discussion at the assignment's conclusion. As student groups work on the assignment, move about the class to listen to their small-group discussions and prompt or redirect their thinking as needed.

Close the Lesson

1. In debriefing the small-group assignment, be sure that students connect the concepts and fully grasp the following concepts:

   • The difference between rate of change in linear and exponential representations

- That both linear and exponential functions represent growth, and that growth can be described as increasing or decreasing
- The symbolic representation for each function
- The characteristics of exponential functions of the form $f(x) = b^x$
  - ▸ The graphs of all exponential functions of the form $f(x) = b^x$ pass through the point $(0, 1)$ because $f(0) = b^0 = 1$ $(b \neq 0)$. The y-intercept is 1.
  - ▸ If $b > 1$, $f(x) = b^x$ has a graph that goes up to the right and is an increasing function. The greater the value of b, the steeper the increase.
  - ▸ If $0 < b < 1$, $f(x) = b^x$ has a graph that goes down to the right and is a decreasing function. The smaller the value of b, the steeper the decrease. *Note:* b cannot be < 0.
  - ▸ The graph of $f(x) = b^x$ approaches, but does not touch, the x-axis. *Note:* Using the term "asymptote" is not required at this point.

2. Help students develop a list of basic characteristics that describe exponential functions. Compare this to the one describing linear functions that was developed at the beginning of the lesson.
3. Close by redirecting the class to the lesson's essential question: "How can growth be represented mathematically?" Ask students to respond to this question in their math notebooks and to set aside a page on which they will list additional real-world examples of exponential growth and decay that they encounter.

Additional Resources for This Lesson

There are several online video clips that can help students better understand exponential growth and its impact on societal and environmental issues, and it would be appropriate to use clips like these as a follow-up to this lesson. The National Council of Teachers of Mathematics website (http://illuminations.nctm.org) also offers activities that could be used to help students build further understanding of exponential functions. In the lesson "Too Hot to Handle, Too Cold to Enjoy" (http://illuminations.nctm.org/LessonDetail.aspx?id=L852), students use temperature probes to collect data as they determine the best point at which to enjoy a hot beverage.

Figure A | **Investigating Linear and Exponential Functions Problem Set**

Work in your small groups to complete the following problems. Remember that everyone in your group should be prepared to contribute to the class debriefing. You may use technology to graph the functions, but be sure to include a sketch of each graph on this page.

1. Complete the table, and graph the functions on the grid.

a. $f(x) = 3x$

x	0	1	2	3
y				

b. $f(x) = 3^x$

x	0	1	2	3
y				

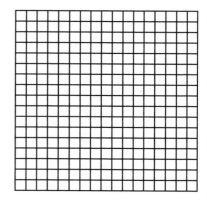

   c. Describe the rate of change in each graph. How does the linear plot compare to the exponential plot?

   d. Why are both of these plots considered growth plots?

2. Complete the table, and graph the functions on the grid.

a. $f(x) = 3 - 2x$

x	0	1	2	3
y				

b. $f(x) = \left(\dfrac{1}{4}\right)^x$

x	0	1	2	3
y				

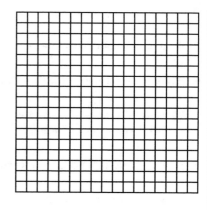

   c. How does each graph change as it approaches the *x*-axis? Explain.

   d. Would the change in the graph be described as increasing or decreasing? Explain.

Figure A | **Investigating Linear and Exponential Functions Problem Set** *(continued)*

3. Describe how the symbolic representation for a linear function compares to the symbolic representation for the exponential function.

   Linear function: $f(x) = 2x$ Exponential function: $f(x) = 2^x$

4. For each of the following, construct a table for the first four points in the plot. Then sketch all functions on the grid. Compare the tables and graph, and then respond to the questions. Graphing technology may be used to confirm graphs.

   a. $f(x) = 2^x$

x	0	1	2	3
y				

   b. $f(x) = 7^x$

x	0	1	2	3
y				

   c. $f(x) = \left(\dfrac{1}{2}\right)^x$

x	0	1	2	3
y				

   d. $f(x) = \left(\dfrac{3}{4}\right)^x$

x	0	1	2	3
y				

   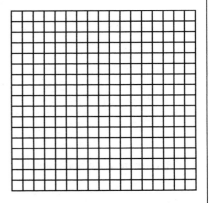

Questions:

5. What do you notice about the y-intercept for each of the graphs? Explain why this occurs.

6. How does the change in the base $(2, 7, \frac{1}{2}, \text{or } \frac{3}{4})$ impact the shape of the graph?

7. Which graphs can be characterized as increasing graphs? Decreasing graphs? How can you predict the direction of the graph by simply looking at the equation?

8. What happens as the graph approaches the x-axis? Explain your reasoning.

9. What is predictable about the graph when $x = 0$? Will this always be true? Explain.

Understanding Conditional Probability

> **Course:** Geometry or Integrated Pathway: Mathematics II
> **Length of Lesson:** Two hours; two 60-minute class periods

Introduction

Although the most obvious application of probability in the world around us occurs in games of chance, probability actually plays an important role in daily life. We use it to make decisions in such diverse fields as weather forecasting, military operations, business predictions, insurance calculations, and the design and quality control of consumer products. The study of probability also helps students build skills for informal decision making. Simply recognizing that insurance rates are substantially higher for teenage drivers (and, in particular, for male teenage drivers) may help students understand how probability directly affects their lives.

According to Appendix A of the Common Core math standards document (CCSSI, 2010d), the study of probability occurs in Geometry (Integrated Pathway: Mathematics II). Although students explore topics in descriptive statistics in grade 8 mathematics and in Algebra I (Integrated Pathway: Mathematics I), most students have few formal learning experiences with probability after grade 7. This is an important consideration when approaching this topic, because teachers may need to plan for additional scaffolding. Prior to adoption of the Common Core, conditional probability was commonly found in college readiness standards, but it was not required curriculum for all students; thus, we can infer that high school teachers may have limited experience teaching these concepts. This lesson offers an introductory approach to the concepts of conditional probability and independence, but students will need other experiences with these concepts to cement their understanding.

Strategies from the Framework for Instructional Planning

- *Creating the Environment for Learning:* The essential questions ("In what situations can the outcome of one event affect the outcome of another?" and "How can understanding probability affect decision making?") and the learning objective ("To develop an understanding of independence and conditional probability and use that understanding to interpret data") are central to the lesson. It is recommended that these statements be posted in the classroom and referred to throughout the lesson. The teacher gives feedback throughout the lesson, and students give feedback to one another. Cooperative learning takes place with informal partnering so that all students have the opportunity to contribute to discussions and learn from one another. A relevant context is used to help students understand how the concepts of this lesson are reflected in situations beyond math class.
- *Helping Students Develop Understanding:* Guided practice, which includes a teacher-prepared handout, is used to help students develop an understanding of the concepts. The handout provides an organized format for note taking and includes tables and diagrams to help students make sense of the data. Nonlinguistic representations are used with the lesson vocabulary, and students are asked to summarize their learning.
- *Helping Students Extend and Apply Knowledge:* Students use data they collect in class to apply their understanding of conditional probability to a new situation. This provides an opportunity for students to generate and test their own hypotheses.

Common Core State Standards—Knowledge and Skills to Be Addressed
Standards for Mathematical Practice

MP4 Model with mathematics.

MP7 Look for and make use of structure.

Standards for Mathematical Content

Conceptual Category/Domain: Statistics and Probability—Conditional Probability and the Rules of Probability

Cluster: Understand Independence and Conditional Probability and Use Them to Interpret Data

HSS-CP.A.4 Construct and interpret two-way frequency tables of data when two categories are associated with each object being classified. Use the two-way table as a sample space to decide if events are independent and to approximate conditional probabilities.

HSS-CP.A.5 Recognize and explain the concepts of conditional probability and independence in everyday language and everyday situations.

Cluster: Use the Rules of Probability to Compute Probabilities of Compound Events in a Uniform Probability Model

HSS-CP.B.6 Find the conditional probability of *A* given *B* as the fraction of *B*'s outcomes that also belong to *A*, and interpret the answer in terms of the model.

Common Core State Standards—Prior Knowledge and Skills to Be Applied

Domain: Statistics and Probability

Cluster: Investigate Chance Processes and Develop, Use, and Evaluate Probability Models
7.SP.C.8 Find probabilities of compound events using organized lists, tables, tree diagrams, and simulation.

   a. Understand that, just as with simple events, the probability of a compound event is the fraction of outcomes in the sample space for which the compound event occurs.
   b. Represent sample spaces for compound events using methods such as organized lists, tables, and tree diagrams.
   c. Design and use a simulation to generate frequencies for compound events.

Conceptual Category/Domain: Statistics and Probability—Conditional Probability and the Rules of Probability

Cluster: Understand Independence and Conditional Probability and Use Them to Interpret Data

HSS-CP.A.1 Describe events as subsets of a sample space (the set of outcomes) using characteristics (or categories) of the outcomes, or as unions, intersections, or complements of other events ("or," "and," "not").

HSS-CP.A.2 Understand that two events A and B are independent if the probability of A and B occurring together is the product of their probabilities, and use this characterization to determine if they are independent.

Teacher's Lesson Summary

This two-day lesson is designed to establish an initial understanding of conditional probability through the use of two-way frequency tables and tree diagrams. Using relevant data, students will be asked to analyze and interpret the data in the context of the problem.

Because this lesson culminates with students analyzing survey data from their own class or school, it will require a fair amount of advance preparation. A week or two before the lesson's scheduled date, work with students to devise survey questions on a topic likely to spark their interest. Topics such as texting and driving, extracurricular activities, teenagers and purchasing habits, or the use of performance-enhancing substances by athletes might be considered. Be sure to collect data that will allow for stratification—for example, male or female, left-handed or right-handed, age spans, and so on. Although collecting the data from one class alone will support the lesson's learning objective, students might find the data more interesting if several classes or the entire school participate in the survey. Data could be collected using tools such as TI-Nspire™ calculators, classroom response systems, class tallies on the board or chart paper, websites such as www.polleverywhere.com, or the Google Docs survey-making option. After the data are collected, ask students to generate hypothesis statements about what the results will show. At the point in the lesson when the survey results are shared, students will compare their predictions to the actual data.

Essential Questions: In what situations can the outcome of one event affect the outcome of another? How can understanding probability impact decision making?
Learning Objective: To develop an understanding of independence and conditional probability and apply it to interpret data.

Knowledge/Vocabulary Objectives
At the conclusion of this lesson, students will

- Understand the relationships between dependent and independent events and conditional probability.

- Understand that probability can be used to explain everyday situations.
- Understand that tables and models are useful for organizing and analyzing data.
- Understand what is meant by conditional probability, independent events, dependent events, a two-way frequency table, and a tree diagram.

Skill/Process Objectives

At the conclusion of this lesson, students will be able to

- Develop a two-way frequency table to organize data.
- Develop a tree diagram to organize data.
- Interpret data within a table or diagram to approximate conditional probability.

Resources/Preparation Needed

1. A handout for the cooperative learning activity on two-way frequency tables (see Figure A, p. 132), one per student
2. A graphic organizer for key vocabulary terms (see Figure B, p. 133), one per student
3. A handout for the guided group learning activity on tree diagrams (see Figure C, pp. 134–135), one per student
4. A handout to guide individual reflection on learning (see Figure D, p. 136), one per student
5. A previously created set of student survey questions and survey results from one or more classes of students—preferably questions students helped develop themselves
6. Student-generated hypothesis statements about the student survey results (e.g., "I expect the data to support the following outcomes . . ."). Students will refer to these statements during the lesson's concluding activity.

Activity Description to Share with Students

Every day, we hear statements that involve probability: "There is a 60 percent chance of rain this evening"; "Four out of five dentists recommend Mighty White toothpaste"; "People who smoke have a greater likelihood of developing cancer than people who don't." Prior experiences with probability helped you understand independence and dependence of events, but this lesson will help you understand what happens when partial information is known. You will continue to use tables and models to organize and interpret information, and you will use the student survey data collected prior to this lesson.

Lesson Activity Sequence—Class #1

Start the Lesson

1. The context for this lesson includes the reading habits of students in grades 4 and 8. Build interest in this topic by providing some background about the National Assessment of Educational Progress (NAEP), and let students know that the academic achievement of U.S. students is an issue that is regularly discussed at the federal, state, and local levels. Share with students that reading achievement has long been studied because it is linked to general academic achievement. Your opening activity should include an explanation of the following situation, adapted from *The Nation's Report Card: Reading 2011* (National Center for Education Statistics, 2011).

   Students in grades 4 and 8 were asked to answer this survey question:

   How often do you read for fun on your own time?
   a. Less than twice per month
   b. At least once per week

   The following information was obtained from grade 4 students:

   • 852 grade 4 students were surveyed.
   • 436 students were female.
   • 242 students responded, "Less than twice per month."

   The following information was obtained from grade 8 students:

   • 914 grade 8 students were surveyed.
   • 468 students were male.
   • 391 students responded, "At least once per week."

2. Ask students to suggest one or more hypotheses for the data, and record these on the board or chart paper for later use. Responses might include, for example,

"Grade 4 students tend to read for fun more often than grade 8 students" or "Male students read for fun less frequently than female students."

3. Engage students in a discussion about how to organize the data. As they offer suggestions, be sure to address any advantages or disadvantages of the models, as appropriate. As the discussion concludes, tell students that a two-way frequency table will be the first method used for organizing the data, and display and distribute the handout for the **Two-Way Frequency Tables Cooperative Learning Activity** (see **Figure A**, p. 132), pointing out the tables it shows.

4. Share the learning objective and essential questions, and keep these posted in the classroom so that you and the students may refer to them during instruction.

Engage Students in Learning the Content

1. Divide students into groups of four for structured collaborative work on the Using Two-Way Frequency Tables handout. The groups should be heterogeneous and include students who work well together. Within each group, two students will collaborate to analyze the grade 4 data, and two students will collaborate to analyze the grade 8 data. Explain to students that they will have approximately 10 minutes to discuss their assigned grade-level data, agree on how to enter it into the two-way frequency table on their personal copy of the handout, and agree on two types of questions for the data set. Remind them that some of the cells in the table will remain blank. Question types include the following:

   • Questions for which there is adequate information in the table to respond. Students should write the question and provide the response. (*Example:* What is the probability that a grade 4 student reads for fun at least once per month? *Response*: 610/852 or .716 or 71.6 percent.)

   • Questions specific to the situation for which there is inadequate information in the table to respond. (*Example:* In grade 4, what is the probability that females read for fun at least once per month versus the probability that males read for fun at least once per month?)

2. Ask the students to share their two-way tables, questions, and responses within their groups of four.

3. After about five minutes, bring the whole class back together and share sample questions as a large group. It is a good idea to display the two-way frequency tables for easy reference and so students can check their accuracy. Check for and address any misconceptions that arise.

4. Draw students' attention to the hypothesis statements they generated earlier in the lesson, and help students understand that more data are needed to answer some of questions. Present the information below:

   Suppose that in grade 4 there were 270 male students that answered, "At least once per week," and in grade 8 there were 164 male students that answered, "At least once per week." What hypotheses could be drawn from this information? (*Example hypothesis*: The probability of a male student reading at least once per week in grade 8 is much smaller than the probability of a male student reading at least once per week in grade 4.)

5. Ask students to fill in the blank cells in their two-way table using the information about male students. When these tables are finished, the original group of four students should work together to answer the following questions on the reverse side of their handout:

   a. What is the probability that a grade 8 female student reads for fun less than twice per month?
   b. What is the probability of a grade 4 student who reads for fun at least once per week being a male student?
   c. What is the probability of a grade 8 student who reads for fun at least once per week being a female student?

6. Ask students to interpret their results and write concluding statements that they can support with their mathematics. Because some students may have limited experience writing concluding statements, it would be helpful to provide sentence starters such as *Based on the data in the two-way tables, it appears ___. This is supported by ___. (Example:* Based on the data in the two-way frequency tables, it appears that as students progress from grade 4 to grade 8, the time that all students spend reading for fun decreases. This is supported by the fact that in grade 4, 71.6 percent of all students read for fun

at least once per week, while in grade 8, only 42.8 percent of all students read for fun at least once per week.)

7. Distribute the **Key Vocabulary for Probability Graphic Organizer** (see **Figure B**, p. 133). Call students' attention to the first term listed, "conditional probability"; explain the concept and ask students to write a definition in the cell provided. Describe the proper notation for conditional probability, and help students understand the "given" in the examples provided. (*Example*: The conditional probability of an event B is the probability that the event will occur given the knowledge that an event A has already occurred. This probability is written $P(B|A)$, notation for the *probability of B given A*.) Once students have written their definition for conditional probability in the chart, ask them to think about an image or words that will help them remember this term. Model this "visualization approach" by sharing a simple drawing that you use to help you remember conditional probability, and describe why it helps you remember. Then ask students to follow a similar process to draw or describe in the space provided how they will remember what conditional probability is.

8. Provide additional practice for proper notation using the information below:

   - Let M represent male students in grade 4.
   - Let F represent female students in grade 4.
   - Let A represent reading for fun at least once per week.
   - Let B represent reading for fun less than twice per month.

   Example question: Suppose you select a grade 4 student at random. What is the probability of selecting a student that reads for fun at least once per week, given the student is a male?

   Notation clarification: $P(A|M)$ is read "the probability of A given M," or in this context, "the probability of selecting a student who reads for fun at least once per week given the student is a male."

   Ask students to provide descriptions and drawings for the remaining words in the Key Vocabulary handout. This work will help students prepare for the next lesson on conditional probability and tree diagrams.

Close the Lesson

1. Ask students to think about the day's lesson and complete the following statement:

   I used to think conditional probability was ____, but now I know that it is ____.

   If time allows, a few student volunteers can share their statements with the whole class.

2. Tell students that that they'll use tree diagrams in the next lesson to learn more about conditional probability.

Lesson Activity Sequence—Class #2

Start the Lesson

Return to the essential questions and learning objective for the lesson. Ask student pairs to discuss these questions using what they learned during the previous class. Provide approximately two minutes for discussion, and then bring the whole group back together. Invite a few volunteers to share what they discussed.

Remind students that tree diagrams can be used to organize and represent data, and let them know that this lesson will use tree diagrams to explore the relationship of independent events and dependent events to conditional probability. Tell students that they will need the work they did in yesterday's class, and allow students time to retrieve their Using Two-Way Frequency Tables and Key Vocabulary handouts.

Engage Students in Learning the Content

1. Distribute the **Tree Diagrams Guided Instruction Handout** (see **Figure C,** pp. 134–135). Using the grade 4 reading data, work with students to develop and interpret tree diagrams displaying the various combinations of student reading habits (e.g., female and reads for fun at least once per week). It may be necessary to help some students set up the tree diagram (e.g., some may not understand that male/female represents the first branch of the tree and reading habits represent the next branches).

2. After the students have identified each branch of the tree and recorded the calculated probabilities from the two-way frequency table, guide them to follow

the branches on the tree diagram to determine the conditional probabilities and interpret the results. A completed tree diagram for the first set of questions might look like this:

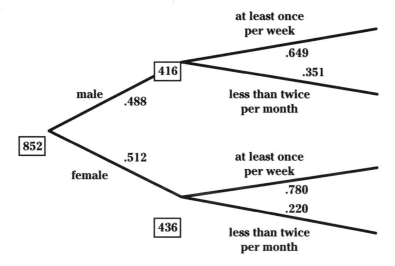

3. *Ask:* Are the events independent? Does the student being male or female affect the probability of the student reading for fun at least once per week or less than twice per month? Prompt students to explain their reasoning and describe how they can use the tree diagram to help determine if two events are independent or dependent. Encourage students to refer to their Key Vocabulary handout and the definitions they wrote for independent and dependent events. (*Independent events:* Events *A* and *B* are said to be independent if neither the probability of *A* nor the probability of *B* is affected by the occurrence of the other event. *Dependent events:* Two events are dependent if the outcome or occurrence of the first affects the outcome or occurrence of the second so that the probability is changed.)

4. Ask students to predict whether the given event changes the outcome of the probability. What is the probability that a student is male given the student reads for fun at least once per week? Would the probability still be .649? Direct students to complete the second tree diagram on the Tree Diagrams handout with the given probability of at least once per week versus less than twice per month and then to calculate and

interpret the conditional probabilities. A completed tree diagram for the second set of questions might look like this:

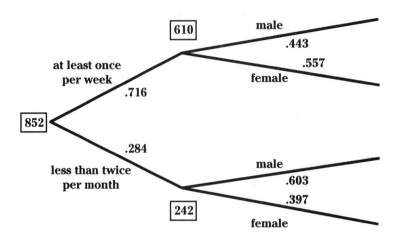

5. The culminating activity for this lesson uses the survey data that were generated by the class; it may be assigned as an individual task or as pair work, and although it should be started during class, it may be completed at home or during the next class session, as appropriate. Present the survey data to the students with information missing, as was done with the practice data on student reading habits. Remind students that they generated hypothesis statements when the survey questions were administered, and ask them to retrieve these statements so that they can make a comparison with the actual data. Direct students to use the data to complete the following tasks:

a. Create a two-way frequency table to organize the class survey results.
b. Calculate all probabilities, including conditional probabilities for the data.
c. Create two tree diagrams to represent the possible conditional probabilities for the survey.
d. Interpret the results and write concluding statements based on the results.
e. Compare the hypotheses statements that you generated to the actual survey results. Were your predictions accurate or inaccurate? Use data to support your statements.
f. Be prepared to share your work in class.

Close the Lesson

1. Distribute the **Reflections on Conditional Probability Handout** (see **Figure D**, p. 136), and give students approximately five minutes to complete its three questions, working independently. Use the remaining class time to share and discuss students' responses.

2. Make sure to allot time during the next lesson to share and discuss the culminating activity.

Additional Resources for This Lesson

The following online resources can be useful for scaffolding or sources for extension activities:

- Kahn Academy tutorials on conditional probability as well as independent and dependent events: www.khanacademy.org
- Stat Trek, "Two-Way Tables in Statistics": http://stattrek.com/ap-statistics-1/association.aspx
- Oswego City School District Regents Exam Prep Center, "Conditional Probability Activity": http://regentsprep.org/REgents/math/ALGEBRA/APR3/Tconditional

Figure A | **Two-Way Frequency Tables Cooperative Learning Activity**

Using Two-Way Frequency Tables to Organize and Present Data

In 2011, students in grades 4 and 8 were asked to answer this survey question:

How often do you read for fun on your own time?
a. Less than twice per month
b. At least once per week

Fourth Grade Student Survey Results: 852 students were surveyed. 436 students were female. 242 students responded, "Less than twice per month."

	Male	Female	Total
Less than twice per month			
At least once per week			
Total			

1. What questions can be answered with these data?

2. What questions cannot be answered because the chart's data are inadequate?

Eigth Grade Student Survey Results: 914 students were surveyed. 468 students were male. 391 students responded, "At least once per week."

	Male	Female	Total
Less than twice per month			
At least once per week			
Total			

1. What questions can be answered with these data?

2. What questions cannot be answered because the chart's data are inadequate?

3. What is a concluding statement that can be made based on the data in the table?

Figure B	**Key Vocabulary for Probability Graphic Organizer**	
Probability Key Term	Definition/Description	Drawing or Description of How You Will Remember This Term
conditional probability		
independent events		
dependent events		
two-way frequency table		
tree diagram		

Figure C | **Tree Diagrams Guided Instruction Handout**

Tree Diagrams: Independent or Dependent Events

Given: Male/Female

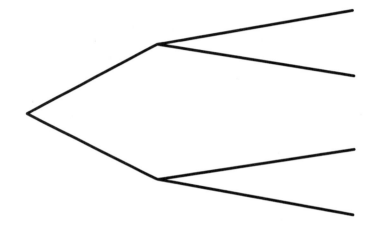

1. Using the tree diagram provided, calculate the conditional probabilities for each of these scenarios.
   a. $P(A|M)$:
   b. $P(A|F)$:
   c. $P(B|M)$:
   d. $P(B|F)$:

2. Are the events in the tree diagram above independent or dependent? That is, does a student being male or female affect the probability of the student reading for fun at least once per week or less than twice per month? Explain your response.

3. Does the tree diagram above prove that all grade 4 females read more often for fun than all grade 4 males? Explain.

Figure C ∣ **Tree Diagrams Guided Instruction Handout** *(continued)*

Given: At Least Once Per Week/Less Than Twice Per Month

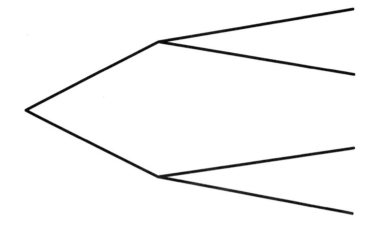

1. Using the tree diagram provided, calculate the conditional probabilities for each of these scenarios.
   a. *P(M∣A)*:
   b. *P(F∣A)*:
   c. *P(M∣B)*:
   d. *P(F∣B)*:

2. How does changing the given condition affect the outcome probability? Explain.

Figure D | **Reflections on Conditional Probability Handout**

Reflecting on Learning

1. Describe how different models (two-way frequency table, tree diagram) are helpful when calculating conditional probability.

2. How can the outcome of one event affect the outcome of another?

3. How can understanding probability influence decision making?

The Unit Circle and Trigonometric Functions

Course: Algebra II or Integrated Pathway: Mathematics III
Length of Lesson: Two hours; two 60-minute class periods

Introduction

According to Appendix A of the Common Core math standards (CCSSI, 2010d), students enrolled in Geometry (Integrated Pathway: Mathematics II) build a foundation for the basic trigonometric functions framed around right triangles. In Algebra II (Integrated Pathway: Mathematics III), students must transition to the unit circle, moving away from right triangle trigonometry to applying the trigonometric functions across the domain of real numbers. This lesson is designed to provide a frame and process to help students build connections between what they already know about right triangles and trigonometric ratios and new learning about the unit circle and radian measures. Prior to the adoption of the Common Core, mastery of this content, common in college readiness standards, was not typically required of all students.

Strategies from the Framework for Instructional Planning

- *Creating the Environment for Learning:* The essential question ("How do the mathematics of trigonometric functions and the unit circle help us solve real-world problems?") and the learning objective ("To develop an understanding of how the unit circle [interpreted as radian measures of an angle] enables the extension of trigonometric functions to all real numbers") are central to the lesson. The teacher gives feedback throughout the lesson, and students give feedback to one another. Cooperative learning takes place with informal partnering, and tasks are assigned based on student readiness for learning. Notice that relevant contexts are provided to help students understand where the concepts they are learning in class are reflected in the world around them.

- *Helping Students Develop Understanding:* This lesson builds on prior knowledge about special right triangles and trigonometric ratios. It incorporates an advance organizer, a unit circle template, and a data table to help students organize their learning. Suggestions for scaffolding learning are included to give teachers a number of options for meeting student needs. Additionally, the questions in the lesson require students to use analytical thinking and to summarize their learning.

- *Helping Students Extend and Apply Knowledge:* This lesson is introductory in nature, but suggestions for extending the learning are provided at the end of the lesson.

Common Core State Standards—Knowledge and Skills to Be Addressed

Standards for Mathematical Practice

MP7 Look for and make use of structure.

Standards for Mathematical Content

Conceptual Category/Domain: Functions—Trigonometric Functions

Cluster: Extend the Domain of Trigonometric Functions Using the Unit Circle

HSF-TF.A.1 Understand radian measure of an angle as the length of the arc on the unit circle subtended by the angle.

HSF-TF.A.2 Explain how the unit circle in the coordinate plane enables the extension of trigonometric functions to all real numbers, interpreted as radian measures of angles traversed counterclockwise around the unit circle.

Common Core State Standards—Prior Knowledge and Skills to Be Applied

Standards for Mathematical Content

Conceptual Category/Domain: Geometry—Similarity, Right Angles, and Trigonometry

Cluster: Define Trigonometric Ratios and Solve Problems Involving Right Triangles

HSG-SRT.C.6 Understand that by similarity, side ratios in right triangles are properties of the angles in the triangle, leading to definitions of trigonometric ratios for acute angles.

HSG-SRT.C.7 Explain and use the relationship between the sine and cosine of complementary angles.

HSG-SRT.C.8 Use trigonometric ratios and the Pythagorean Theorem to solve right triangles in applied problems.

Teacher's Lesson Summary

Over the course of two class sessions, students explore the unit circle, radian measures, and trigonometric functions. The first session focuses on making connections between students' prior knowledge of special right triangles and trigonometric functions to build an understanding of the unit circle. Through discussion and exploration, students learn how the unit circle can extend the trigonometric functions to all real numbers.

The second session expands the focus to the measurement of angles along the unit circle in radians as well as to applications of the unit circle. Students' attention is called to how the mathematics they are learning connects to postsecondary career fields such as physics and civil engineering.

Essential Question: How do the mathematics of trigonometric functions and the unit circle help us solve real-world problems?

Learning Objective: To develop an understanding of how the unit circle (interpreted as radian measures of an angle) enables the extension of trigonometric functions to all real numbers.

Knowledge/Vocabulary Objectives

At the conclusion of this lesson, students will

- Understand radian measure as the length of the arc on the unit circle subtended by the angle.

- Understand how measurement with radians differs from measurement with degrees.
- Understand how the unit circle enables the extension of trigonometric functions to all real numbers.

Skill/Process Objectives

At the conclusion of this lesson, students will be able to

- Explain how the unit circle enables the extension of trigonometric functions to all real numbers.
- Recognize and/or draw a radian measure in a unit circle.
- Determine the measure of an angle in the unit circle using radian measurement.
- Determine the value of the trigonometric functions (sine, cosine, and tangent) for given angle measures with reference to the unit circle.
- Compare similarities and differences of degree and radian measurements for angles in the unit circle by identifying patterns.

Resources/Preparation Needed

- An advance organizer for the topic of trigonometric functions (see Figure A, p. 150), one per student
- A handout for a guided learning activity on the unit circle (see Figure B, pp. 151–152), one per student
- Two application tasks, differentiated by readiness (see Figure D, p. 154, and Figure E, p. 155), one per student

Activity Description to Share with Students

In this two-day lesson, you will discover how what you already know about trigonometric functions applies to finding the sine, cosine, and tangent of angles not found in a right triangle. You will explore the unit circle and learn how to find angle measures in radians rather than degrees. You'll also learn more about what types of career fields use these mathematical concepts.

Lesson Activity Sequence—Class #1

Start the Lesson

1. Post the learning objective and share the essential question. Encourage discussion about the essential question, and then tell students that the objective

will be addressed during two class sessions. During the first session, they will be focusing on the unit circle and how to use it to determine angle measures; in the second lesson, they will focus on applications of trigonometric functions.

2. Access and build on students' prior knowledge. Divide the class into groups of four to five, and give each student a copy of the **Trigonometric Functions Advance Organizer** (see **Figure A**, p. 150). Assign groups one trigonometric function each, and provide approximately two minutes for group members to brainstorm characteristics of the function (e.g., how to find the sine of an angle using right triangle trigonometry). Have groups share their ideas with the entire class; clarify any misconceptions that surface. Direct students to record information they learn from members of other groups on their own advance organizers so that they have lists of characteristics for each function.

3. Once a discussion of sine, cosine, and tangent functions has taken place, ask students to independently answer the first reflection question on the advance organizer: What are characteristics that all three functions have in common? (Answers might include that the value of each trigonometric function can be found by using a ratio of two sides of a right triangle.)

4. Display the triangle shown below, and ask student pairs to discuss the following questions:

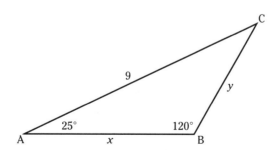

- Could a trigonometric function be used to find the missing side lengths of this triangle? Explain.
- How could you determine the sine of a non-positive angle?

Lead a class discussion that helps students grasp that their prior knowledge of trigonometric functions makes sense only for right triangles. Then remind them about special right triangles, such as the 45°- 45°- 90° and 30°- 60°- 90° ones shown here:

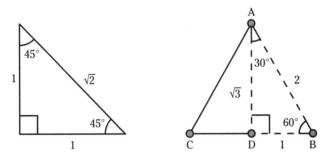

Tell students that this lesson will help them extend their knowledge of special right triangles and trigonometric functions to all real numbers. This understanding will allow them to find the sine, cosine, or tangent for angle measures that are not acute and even for angle measures that are non-positive.

Engage Students in Learning the Content

1. Introduce students to the unit circle by drawing the 45°- 45°- 90° special right triangle in Quadrant I of the unit circle, like so:

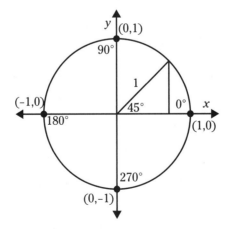

Discuss with students that this 45°- 45°- 90° triangle may differ from the ones they have formerly used, since the hypotenuse now measures one unit, based upon the definition of a unit circle. Discuss the various characteristics of the triangle, including side lengths of the triangle, values of the trigonometric functions, and the coordinate of the endpoint that lies on the unit circle. Next, move the 45°- 45°- 90° special right triangle into Quadrant II and discuss the characteristics of the new triangle.

2. Distribute copies of the **Unit Circle Template and Data Table Guided Group Learning Handout** (see **Figure B**, pp. 151–152). Walk students through the completion for both special right triangles located in Quadrants I and II, conveying the following information:

- **Unit Circle Understandings:**
  - ▸ The unit circle is a circle on the coordinate plane with a center at (0, 0) and a radius of one unit.
  - ▸ Angles within the unit circle are measured by starting on the positive *x*-axis at point (1, 0) and moving counterclockwise along the circle.
  - ▸ Endpoints lie on the unit circle.

- **Special Right Triangles Understandings:**
  - ▸ The length of the hypotenuse is one unit.
  - ▸ Knowledge of special right triangles and the Pythagorean Theorem can be used to identify the coordinates that lie on the unit circle and to find the sine, cosine, and tangent of the angle (see Example A).

Example A

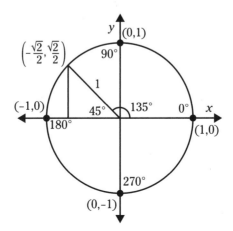

▸ The coordinates on the unit circle can be compared to trigonometric functions to identify patterns.

▸ Clockwise movement on the unit circle from point (1,0) results in an angle measurement that is not positive (e.g., an angle measuring 45° on the unit circle shares a terminal side with an angle measuring –315°; see Example B).

Example B

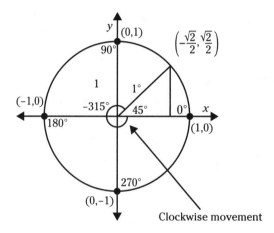

▸ Multiple revolutions around the unit circle result in an angle measure greater than 360° (see Example C).

Example C

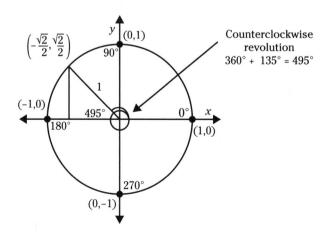

3. Ask students to work individually or in pairs to complete their copies of the Unit Circle Template and Data Table handout for Quadrants III and IV. (*Note:* Students will not complete the "Angle Measure in Radians" column on the data table or the radian measurements on the Unit Circle Template until the following class session.) Make sure that students understand how their prior knowledge can be extended to find the sine, cosine, and tangent for angle measures that are not acute and not positive. When students have completed the first class session work on the Unit Circle Template, they should work in pairs to identify patterns related to the coordinates on the unit circle. Circulate through the classroom to check on students' work, making sure to clarify any misconceptions.

Close the Lesson

Conclude the lesson by asking students to refer to their advance organizer and answer reflection questions #2 and #3. Allow a few minutes for students to share their responses with a classmate. Finally, ask students to individually write questions they still have about the unit circle and trigonometric functions on a sticky note and post the note before leaving class. Explain that these questions will help guide your instruction during the next class session.

Lesson Activity Sequence—Class #2

Start the Lesson

Remind students of the essential question and learning objective. Tell them that they will use the information from the previous day's class to solve problems. Then, as a whole class, go through the questions students posted at the end of Class #1, providing answers and correcting any apparent misconceptions.

Engage Students in Learning the Content

1. Elicit students' prior knowledge about circumference ($C = 2\pi r$) and arc length, and ask students to find the circumference of the unit circle.
2. Lead students to understand that one revolution around the unit circle is equal to 2π or 360°.
3. Help students make connections between degrees, radians, and revolutions by identifying both radian and degree measures for one-quarter, one-half, and

three-quarter revolutions. Then ask students to work in pairs to complete the radian measures on the Unit Circle Template and Data Table handout. When they've completed their work, provide them with a copy of the **Unit Circle Data Table Answer Key** (see **Figure C**, p. 153). so that they can check and discuss their responses. Ask them to describe the patterns they notice in the radian measures on the unit circle.

4. Help students understand applications of radian measure beyond mathematics class, using the following examples, if desired:

> Artists frequently use mathematics to help create visually appealing pieces. According to Anne M. Burns, the unit circle is a subgroup of the group of Mobius Transformations. Read about how the image at right and other circle images are created at www.anneburns.net/circles/unitcircle.html.

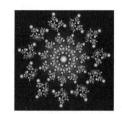

> Civil engineers use the unit circle and arc lengths in road design. Suppose you are given a site plan of two roads in an area of recent home construction growth and increased traffic. The state would like to add an interchange to the highway. The best option is to create a circular ramp, like those illustrated here. You will need to find the arc length of the ramp to determine the length of road to be built and paved in an effort to estimate cost and create a detailed site plan for workers.

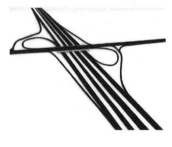

At this time, you may also choose to use the common student questions posed in the "Additional Resources" section (see p. 147) to help build students' understanding of radian measurement and the unit circle.

5. Move on to an application assignment differentiated by readiness. Students who are ready to work independently should complete the **Analog Clock Application Task** (see **Figure D**, p. 154), answering the questions in the handout. Students in need of direct teacher support should work first with you in a mini-lesson arrangement to complete the **Ride Design Guided Application Task** (see **Figure E**, p. 155), answering the questions listed in the handout and

any other questions you pose. After these students have developed confidence with these skills, they might complete the Analog Clock task for independent practice.

Close the Lesson

1. Ask students to reflect on the learning from the last two class sessions and then share with a partner (1) one concept that they feel they understand well enough to teach it to someone else and (2) one concept that they don't quite understand. Ask students to share these thoughts as a whole class so that both you and the students themselves can discover where additional instruction, support, or practice is needed.
2. Return to the lesson's essential question, and direct students to respond to the question in their notebook.

Additional Resources for This Lesson

Common Student Questions

Q: Why can't we just measure in degrees?

A: Degrees can be used to measure the angle, but when working with advanced concepts, calculations become quite messy. This makes measuring in radians a simpler alternative. Radians represent "slices" of π, and the relationship of radians to circumference helps us better understand arc length, or distance along the circle.

Q: Does the radius of a unit circle have to be 1?

A: By definition the unit circle must have a radius of 1. To help you think about this, consider the properties of the unit circle but change the radius to 2. How would this affect our angle measures in degrees? In radians? How would sine, cosine, and tangent be affected? What *is* affected, then?

Q: Why is it important to learn about the unit circle and radians?

A: The unit circle and radians will be helpful as you move to application problems involving rotations or revolutions. The diagrams and chart here can help you make the connections between degrees, radians, and revolutions:

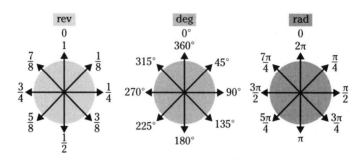

words	rev	deg	rad
no turn	0	0°	0
quarter turn	$\frac{1}{4}$	90°	$\frac{\pi}{2}$
half turn	$\frac{1}{2}$	180°	π
three-quarter turn	$\frac{3}{4}$	270°	$\frac{3\pi}{2}$
full turn	1	360°	2π
twelfth turn	$\frac{1}{12}$	30°	$\frac{\pi}{6}$
eighth turn	$\frac{1}{8}$	45°	$\frac{\pi}{4}$
sixth turn	$\frac{1}{6}$	60°	$\frac{\pi}{3}$
fifth turn	$\frac{1}{5}$	72°	$\frac{2\pi}{5}$
third turn	$\frac{1}{3}$	120°	$\frac{2\pi}{3}$
two turns	2	720°	4π
three turns	3	1080°	6π

Websites

- Khan Academy, "Unit Circle Definition of Trig Functions: Using the Unit Circle to Define the Sine, Cosine, and Tangent Functions" (online video): www.khanacademy .org/video/unit-circle-definition-of-trig-functions? playlist=Trigonometry

- NCTM, "Graphs from the Unit Circle" (lesson plan): http://illuminations.nctm.org/LessonDetail.aspx?id=L785
- NCTM, "Rolling into Radians" (lesson plan): http://illuminations.nctm.org/LessonDetail.aspx?id=L844

Extension Task

An extension task from Texas Instruments that includes the use of graphing technology and provides another application of the unit circle is available online at http://education.ti.com/xchange/US/Math/PrecalculusTrig/13451/Application_of_the_Unit_Circle_Student.pdf (student activity) and http://education.ti.com/xchange/US/Math/PrecalculusTrig/13451/Application_of_the_Unit_Circle_Teacher.pdf (teacher notes).

Figure A | **Trigonometric Functions Advance Organizer**

Trigonometric Functions

Use the space below to list characteristics of each trigonometric function. Each group will be assigned one trigonometric function and report on it to the rest of the class. Be sure to capture on this sheet the information from other groups as they present their assigned function.

Sine Function	Cosine Function	Tangent Function

Reflection Questions

1. What are characteristics that all three functions have in common?

2. As a result of today's work, what new information have you learned? What patterns did you observe?

3. Why do you suppose it is important to extend our knowledge of sine, cosine, and tangent beyond acute angle measures?

Figure B | **Unit Circle Template and Data Table Guided Group Learning Handout**

As a class, we will work together to identify the coordinate points, angle degrees, and radian measurements on the unit circle. Radian measurements will be added during Class #2.

Fill in the Unit Circle

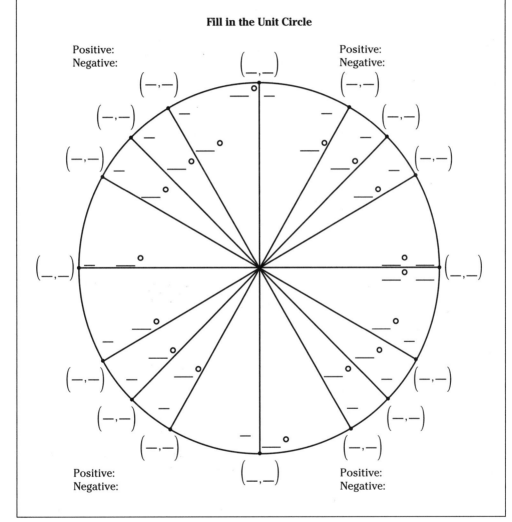

Figure B	**Unit Circle Template and Data Table Guided Group Learning Handout** *(continued)*							
We will work to complete this data table as a class. Angle measures in radians will be added during Class #2.								
Corresponding Special Right Triangle	Angle Measure in Degrees	Corresponding Non-positive Angle Measure	Angle Measure in Radians	Trigonometric Functions			Coordinate on the Unit Circle	
				Sin	Cos	Tan		
	0°							
	90°							
	180°							
	270°							
45°- 45°- 90°								
45°- 45°- 90°								
45°- 45°- 90°								
45°- 45°- 90°								
30°- 60°- 90°								
30°- 60°- 90°								
30°- 60°- 90°								
30°- 60°- 90°								
30°- 60°- 90°								
30°- 60°- 90°								
30°- 60°- 90°								
30°- 60°- 90°								

Figure C ǀ **Unit Circle Data Table Answer Key**							
Corresponding Special Right Triangle	Angle Measure in Degrees	Corresponding Non-positive Angle Measure	Angle Measure in Radians	Trigonometric Functions			Coordinate on the Unit Circle
				Sin	Cos	Tan	
	0°		0	0	1	0	$(1, 0)$
	90°	−270°	$\frac{\pi}{2}$	1	0	—	$(0, 1)$
	180°	−180°	π	0	−1	0	$(−1, 0)$
	270°	−90°	$\frac{3\pi}{2}$	−1	0	—	$(0, −1)$
45°- 45°- 90°	45°	−315°	$\frac{\pi}{4}$	$\frac{\sqrt{2}}{2}$	$\frac{\sqrt{2}}{2}$	1	$\left(\frac{\sqrt{2}}{2}, \frac{\sqrt{2}}{2}\right)$
45°- 45°- 90°	135°	−225°	$\frac{3\pi}{4}$	$\frac{\sqrt{2}}{2}$	$-\frac{\sqrt{2}}{2}$	−1	$\left(-\frac{\sqrt{2}}{2}, \frac{\sqrt{2}}{2}\right)$
45°- 45°- 90°	225°	−135°	$\frac{5\pi}{4}$	$-\frac{\sqrt{2}}{2}$	$-\frac{\sqrt{2}}{2}$	1	$\left(-\frac{\sqrt{2}}{2}, -\frac{\sqrt{2}}{2}\right)$
45°- 45°- 90°	315°	−45°	$\frac{7\pi}{4}$	$-\frac{\sqrt{2}}{2}$	$\frac{\sqrt{2}}{2}$	−1	$\left(\frac{\sqrt{2}}{2}, -\frac{\sqrt{2}}{2}\right)$
30°- 60°- 90°	30°	−330°	$\frac{\pi}{6}$	$\frac{1}{2}$	$\frac{\sqrt{3}}{2}$	$\frac{\sqrt{3}}{3}$	$\left(\frac{\sqrt{3}}{2}, \frac{1}{2}\right)$
30°- 60°- 90°	60°	−300°	$\frac{\pi}{3}$	$\frac{\sqrt{3}}{2}$	$\frac{1}{2}$	$\sqrt{3}$	$\left(\frac{1}{2}, \frac{\sqrt{3}}{2}\right)$
30°- 60°- 90°	120°	−240°	$\frac{2\pi}{3}$	$\frac{\sqrt{3}}{2}$	$-\frac{1}{2}$	$-\sqrt{3}$	$\left(-\frac{1}{2}, \frac{\sqrt{3}}{2}\right)$
30°- 60°- 90°	150°	−210°	$\frac{5\pi}{6}$	$\frac{1}{2}$	$-\frac{\sqrt{3}}{2}$	$-\frac{\sqrt{3}}{3}$	$\left(-\frac{\sqrt{3}}{2}, \frac{1}{2}\right)$
30°- 60°- 90°	210°	−150°	$\frac{7\pi}{6}$	$-\frac{1}{2}$	$-\frac{\sqrt{3}}{2}$	$\frac{\sqrt{3}}{3}$	$\left(-\frac{\sqrt{3}}{2}, -\frac{1}{2}\right)$
30°- 60°- 90°	240°	−120°	$\frac{4\pi}{3}$	$-\frac{\sqrt{3}}{2}$	$-\frac{1}{2}$	$\sqrt{3}$	$\left(-\frac{1}{2}, -\frac{\sqrt{3}}{2}\right)$
30°- 60°- 90°	300°	−60°	$\frac{5\pi}{3}$	$-\frac{\sqrt{3}}{2}$	$\frac{1}{2}$	$-\sqrt{3}$	$\left(\frac{1}{2}, -\frac{\sqrt{3}}{2}\right)$
30°- 60°- 90°	330°	−30°	$\frac{11\pi}{6}$	$-\frac{1}{2}$	$\frac{\sqrt{3}}{2}$	$-\frac{\sqrt{3}}{3}$	$\left(\frac{\sqrt{3}}{2}, -\frac{1}{2}\right)$

Figure D | **Analog Clock Application Task**

Your task is to design a 12-hour circular analog clock. Each digit will be equally spaced, with the 12 at the topmost position.

Sketch a diagram of the clock, labeling each hour with the degree measure and radian measure that correspond to that hour's position. Draw the *x*-axis through the 9 and 3 and the *y*-axis through the 12 and 6. Use the sketch to answer the questions.

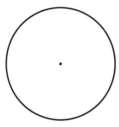

1. If the hour hand is at the measure indicated below, what hour does the clock read?

   a. 300°   b. –210°   c. $\frac{\pi}{3}$ d. $\frac{-11\pi}{6}$

2. If the clock hands are at the indicated locations below, what time does the clock read?

   a. Hour hand is at 120°; minute hand is at –120°.

   b. Hour hand is at $\frac{-\pi}{6}$; minute hand is at $\frac{4\pi}{3}$.

3. What is the radius of your clock design? Using the radius, what is the arc length between each hour on the clock?

4. What are the angle measure (degrees and radians) and the arc length between the 2 and the 9 on your clock? (*Hint:* Remember to rotate counterclockwise from the *x*-axis.)

5. Explain how the unit circle enables you to find the sine, cosine, and tangent of angle measures that are non-positive and angle measures that are not acute.

Figure E | **Ride Design Guided Application Task**

Our task: Design an amusement park ride that consists of eight rotating cars placed on a circular base. We want to make sure that the eight cars are spaced evenly around the circumference of the base to maintain balance during operation.

Following along with the teacher, in the space below, draw a sketch of the ride noting the location of each cart in radians and degrees. Number the carts 1–8, positioning cart 1 at 0° and proceeding counterclockwise with the remaining carts.

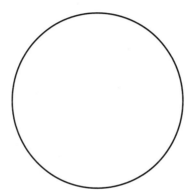

Questions

1. Which cart is located at 135°?

2. Which cart is located at $\frac{-7\pi}{4}$?

3. If the radius of the circular base is 8 feet, what is the circumference of the base?

4. If the radius of the base is 8 feet, what is the distance along the base's circumference between cart 2 and cart 5 (arc length)?

References

Common Core State Standards Initiative. (2010a). *Application of Common Core State Standards for English language learners*. Washington, DC: CCSSO & National Governors Association. Retrieved from http://www.corestandards.org/assets/application-for-english-learners.pdf

Common Core State Standards Initiative. (2010b). *Application to students with disabilities*. Washington, DC: CCSSO & National Governors Association. Retrieved from http://www.corestandards.org/assets/application-to-students-with-disabilities.pdf

Common Core State Standards Initiative. (2010c). *Common Core State Standards for mathematics*. Washington, DC: CCSSO & National Governors Association. Retrieved from http://www.corestandards.org/assets/CCSSI_Math%20Standards.pdf

Common Core State Standards Initiative. (2010d). *Common Core State Standards for mathematics. Appendix A: Designing high school mathematics courses based on the Common Core State Standards*. Washington, DC: CCSSO & National Governors Association. Retrieved from http://www.corestandards.org/assets/CCSSI_Mathematics_Appendix_A.pdf

Dean, C. B., Hubbell, E. R., Pitler, H., & Stone, B. (2012). *Classroom instruction that works: Research-based strategies for increasing student achievement* (2nd ed.). Alexandria, VA: ASCD.

Kendall, J. S. (2011). *Understanding Common Core State Standards*. Alexandria, VA: ASCD.

National Center for Education Statistics. (2011). *The Nation's Report Card: Reading 2011* (NCES 2012-457). National Assessment of Educational Progress. Washington, DC: U.S. Department of Education, Institute of Education Sciences.

National Research Council, Committee on a Conceptual Framework for New K–12 Science Education Standards. (2012). *A framework for K–12 science education: Practices, crosscutting concepts, and core ideas.* Washington, DC: National Academies Press. Retrieved from http://www.nap.edu/openbook.php?record_id=13165&page=1

National Research Council, Committee on How People Learn: A Targeted Report for Teachers. (2005). *How students learn: Mathematics in the classroom.* Washington, DC: National Academies Press.

Partnership for Assessment of Readiness for College and Careers. (2011). *PARCC model content frameworks: Mathematics, grades 3–11.* Retrieved from http://www.parcconline.org/sites/parcc/files/PARCC%20MCF%20for%20Mathematics_Fall%202011%20Release.pdf

About the Authors

Amitra Schwols serves as a consultant at Mid-continent Research for Education and Learning (McREL). As an analyst at McREL, she has reviewed, revised, and developed standards documents for many districts, state agencies, and organizations. She has also reviewed instructional materials, created lesson plans, and conducted research on a wide variety of education topics. Ms. Schwols's work with the Common Core State Standards includes developing gap analysis, crosswalk, and transition documents, as well as facilitating implementation with groups of teacher leaders. She was a consulting state content expert for mathematics during the development of the Common Core standards and a state consultant to the Partnership for Assessment of Readiness for College and Careers (PARCC) consortium. A former classroom teacher at the secondary grades and a Navy veteran, Ms. Schwols holds a BS in science with an emphasis in physics and mathematics and a minor in English from Colorado State University.

Kathleen Dempsey is a principal consultant with McREL. In this role, Ms. Dempsey works to provide services, strategies, and materials to support improvement in mathematics education, curriculum development, formative assessment, and integration of instructional technology. Additionally, Ms. Dempsey currently serves as a primary investigator for two mathematics studies funded by the Institute of Education Sciences. Ms. Dempsey holds an MEd in educational supervision from the College of William and Mary, a BS in elementary education from Old Dominion University, and endorsements in mathematics—Algebra I, gifted education, and middle school education. Before coming to McREL, Ms. Dempsey served as the secondary mathematics coordinator for Virginia Beach City Public Schools in Virginia Beach, Virginia.

John Kendall (Series Editor) is Senior Director in Research at McREL in Denver. Having joined McREL in 1988, Mr. Kendall conducts research and development activities related to academic standards. He directs a technical assistance unit that provides standards-related services to schools, districts, states, and national and international organizations. He is the author of *Understanding Common Core State Standards,* the senior author of *Content Knowledge: A Compendium of Standards and Benchmarks for K–12 Education,* and the author or coauthor of numerous reports and guides related to standards-based systems. These works include *High School Standards and Expectations for College and the Workplace, Essential Knowledge: The Debate over What American Students Should Know,* and *Finding the Time to Learn: A Guide.* He holds an MA in Classics and a BA in English Language and Literature from the University of Colorado at Boulder.

About McREL

McREL is a nationally recognized nonprofit education research and development organization headquartered in Denver, Colorado, with offices in Honolulu, Hawaii, and Omaha, Nebraska. Since 1966, McREL has helped translate research and professional wisdom about what works in education into practical guidance for educators. Our more than 120 staff members and affiliates include respected researchers, experienced consultants, and published writers who provide educators with research-based guidance, consultation, and professional development for improving student outcomes.

ASCD and Common Core State Standards Resources

ASCD believes that for the Common Core State Standards to have maximum effect, they need to be part of a well-rounded whole child approach to education that ensures students are healthy, safe, engaged, supported, and challenged.

For a complete and updated overview of ASCD's resources related to the Common Core standards, including other Quick-Start Guides in the Understanding the Common Core Standards Series, professional development institutes, online courses links to webinars and to ASCD's free EduCore™ digital tool, and lots more, please visit us at **www.ascd.org/commoncore**.